OFFENSIVE AND DEFENSIVE LAWFARE:

FIGHTING CIVILIZATION JIHAD IN AMERICA'S COURTS

CIVILIZATION JIHAD READER SERIES

Volume 7

ISBN-13: 978-1518657504

ISBN-10: 1518657508

Offensive and Defensive Lawfare: Fighting Civilization Jihad in America's Courts is published in the United States by the Center for Security Policy Press, a division of the Center for Security Policy.

October 16, 2015

THE CENTER FOR SECURITY POLICY
1901 Pennsylvania Avenue, Suite 201 Washington, DC 20006
Phone: (202) 835-9077 | Email: info@securefreedom.org
For more information, please see securefreedom.org

Book design by Adam Savit and Brittany Clift
Cover design by Alex VanNess

TABLE OF CONTENTS

FOREWORD

Lawfare – the use of litigation and other judicial instruments to achieve policy outcomes – has long been employed by the U.S. progressive movement. In recent years, it has become a favored weapon of the Left's allies in the Muslim Brotherhood and other parts of the global jihad movement in America.

In particular, organizations in this country that front for the Brotherhood and its Palestinian franchise, Hamas, such as the Council on American Islamic Relations (CAIR), have wielded lawfare both strategically and tactically. Their focus typically involves efforts to create and promote victimization narratives for Islam. They seek to silence their critics and put the American public and policy-makers on the defensive in the face of the global and domestic threat from a jihad or holy war, driven by the dictates of the Islamic supremacist doctrine known as shariah.

In advancing this agenda, the Muslim Brotherhood uses our own laws and courts for such purposes as intimidating and otherwise suppressing any who dare challenge Islamic supremacism. A steady stream of lawsuits filed by Muslims in this country works to achieve such outcomes and to normalize shariah by: insinuating it incrementally into our legal system; advancing the claim that Islamic law ought to be treated as superior to our basic freedoms; and gaining acceptance for anti-constitutional Islamic tenets related to equality, women's rights, free speech and more.

One of the nation's leading, most steadfast and supremely skilled opponents of such lawfare is David Yerushalmi, Esq. Mr. Yerushalmi is the co-founder and Senior Counsel of the American Freedom Law Center, a public interest law firm specializing in pro bono representation of exponents of religious and other freedoms. He also serves as the General Counsel for the Center for Security Policy and is the author of this important new contribution to the Center's Civilization Jihad Reader Series: *Lawfare: The Jihad's Use of Litigation to Undermine American Freedoms – and How to Defeat It.*

As important as David Yerushalmi's accounts of how the jihadists wage lawfare against American and such liberties as freedom of speech are his recommendations about an *offensive* lawfare strategy for defending the U.S. Constitution and our legal system from any further encroachment by Islamic law.

Given accelerating attempts by the shariah forces to advance their agenda, this monograph could hardly be more timely. Nor could the topic have found a better champion to lay out this pro-democracy, countervailing lawfare strategy than Mr. Yerushalmi – a brilliant attorney who specializes in litigation and risk analysis, especially as it relates to geo-strategic policy, national security, international business relations, securities law, disclosure and due diligence requirements for domestic and international concerns. He is also an experienced combatant in the lawfare wars with CAIR and other entities – governmental and private sector – that seek to enable, or at least excuse, the perpetrators of what the Muslim Brotherhood calls "civilization jihad."

With this new monograph, the Center for Security Policy hopes to underscore the importance of the lawfare battlespace to defending the Constitution and foundational American principles against shariah. Mr. Yerushalmi, along with co-author and co-founder of the American Freedom Law Center, Robert J. Muise, Esq., has provided us an initial blueprint on how to use the courts, both defensively and offensively, to thwart the shariah threat.

There is much material to master here, aside from shariah itself: Those who decide to enter this arena will likely be staking out new initiatives, by applying techniques peculiar to this legal battlespace. They must also understand that such initiatives will likely be sharply challenged. If past experience is any guide, our shariah-adherent opponents will use every method at their disposal to attack those who oppose the Brotherhood's agenda, including defamation, lawsuits naming legal counsel, motions for sanctions and the like.

We at the Center and our pioneering legal colleagues, like Mssrs. Yerushalmi and Muise, are convinced that we nonetheless have no choice but to counter the jihadists' lawfare and to wage it effectively in our own right in defense of the Constitution and the people whose freedoms it guarantees.

We hope this monograph will serve as a wake-up call for the courts, judges, lawyers and legislators – and, indeed, for all those engaged in the public policy debate. It is meant to help them recognize that acquiescing to the jihadists' lawfare would be tantamount to an intolerable abdication of our duty as citizens to defend the Constitution against all enemies, foreign and domestic and a call to arms to encourage and equip them, instead, to perform that solemn duty.

Frank J. Gaffney, Jr.
President and CEO
Center for Security Policy

INTRODUCTION

This monograph will explain at the theoretical level what lawfare is and how it is used in practice by the Muslim Brotherhood, its affiliates, and its secular progressive allies in government to wage civilization jihad. This alliance—often passive but sometimes quite assertive—of Muslim "civil rights" organizations and progressives in and out of government works as a *de facto* juggernaut, which seeks to disarm and denude any criticism of shariah-driven political Islam. The ultimate purpose for the Brotherhood is to pave the way for governmental policies that serve as anti-blasphemy laws mirroring the growing demand that any criticism of shariah-centered Islam should be self-censored, and, if that fails, censored by the courts and the executive branches of state and federal governments. The progressives find this agenda quite useful in forcing upon the West a defensive posture, putting the West's nation-states on the defensive and without a strong voice to defend the homeland or to assert a national sovereignty predicated upon exceptionalism (*i.e.*, the United States) or upon a strong national culture (*i.e.*, European and Scandinavian countries).

We will also detail a counter program, sometimes referred to as "counter-lawfare," that utilizes lawfare itself to defend against the Brotherhood-Progressive agenda, and indeed, to go on the offensive to attack the efforts to redefine our constitutionally-protected liberty of free speech into a version of Europe's replete with "hate speech" prohibitions that work to criminalize criticism of Islam. The American Freedom Law Center (AFLC), a nonprofit public interest law firm, which operates in cooperation with the Center for Security Policy (CSP), has stepped into this arena to defend against the Brotherhood-Progressive lawfare agenda and to bring an offensive capability to dismantle the juggernaut at the point of contact in the courts.

WHAT IS "LAWFARE"?

As used here, "lawfare" refers to the use of the American judicial system to influence and ultimately change public policy. In short, it is the use of litigation and the threat of litigation to achieve policy ends. Indeed, for good or ill, the courts have historically provided unique opportunities to change public policy, as we have observed through the litigation advanced over the years by various "rights" groups and activists. The same is true in this fight against civilization jihad. The proponents of civilization jihad are directly engaged in lawfare to achieve their goal of subverting our political system and the freedoms it guarantees, and we, the opponents of civilization jihad, are defending against such attacks as well as launching our own offensive to ensure that our freedoms remain intact.

There are three basic goals of lawfare. First, strategically, lawfare seeks to directly change public policy by way of favorable court rulings or binding settlements. Second, tactically, lawfare seeks to change the behavior of government officials through litigation or the threat of litigation without ever achieving a favorable ruling. With lawfare, victory does not necessarily require a favorable court judgment. The cost of litigation in terms of time, finances, and media exposure has the potential to influence behavior as effectively as a court ruling. And finally, a critical goal of lawfare is to influence and shape public discourse to ultimately influence and shape public opinion. Changing public opinion is often a prerequisite to changing public policy. Litigation creates earned media and thus provides an excellent opportunity to engage the public through this media. Indeed, the drama of a courtroom setting attracts public attention and thereby provides a forum and an audience for expressing the appropriate public policy narrative.

How Lawfare Is Used to Promote and Counter Civilization Jihad

It can no longer be plausibly denied that the Muslim Brotherhood and its affiliated organizations are engaging in civilization jihad in America. And the Muslim Brotherhood organization leading this charge in the lawfare arena is the Council on American-Islamic Relations (CAIR), which holds itself out to the public and to the courts as the nation's leading public interest organization defending the civil rights of Muslims.[1]

The Muslim Brotherhood's strategic plan for North America is found in a document entitled, *An Explanatory Memorandum: On the General Strategic Goal for the Group*, which was written in 1991 by Mohammed Akram, a member of the Board of Directors for the Muslim Brotherhood in North America and a senior Hamas leader. This document, which was introduced by the federal government in the Holy Land Foundation terrorism financing trial, the largest of its kind to date that resulted in criminal convictions,[2] was subsequently approved by the Muslim Brotherhood's Shura Council and Organizational Conference, and it sets forth the mission of the Muslim Brotherhood in America as follows:

The process of settlement is a 'Civilization Jihadist Process' with all the word means. The [Muslim Brotherhood] must understand their work in America is a kind of grand jihad in eliminating and destroying the Western civilization from within and 'sabotaging' its miserable house by their hands and the hands of the believers so that it is eliminated and God's religion is made victorious over all other religions.

The Muslim Brotherhood's goal of "eliminating and destroying [America] from within" is a direct reference to the use of lawfare—that is, the Muslim Brotherhood is committed to using America's legal system to advance shariah and Islamic supremacy and to punish those who oppose it. We turn now to some concrete examples.

---

[1] *See, e.g.*, https://cair.com/civil-rights.html.

[2] CAIR, among others, was an unindicted co-conspirator in the Holy Land Foundation case. *See United States v. Holy Land Found. for Relief & Dev.*, 624 F.3d 685, 689 n.1 (5th Cir. 2010).

Defamation Lawsuits

A common tactic of those wishing to suppress the right to freedom of speech, or more specifically, suppress the right to publicly oppose Islam and the Muslim Brotherhood's agenda, is to file (or threaten to file) a defamation lawsuit. This tactic serves multiple purposes. First, it frequently results in the silencing of the lawsuit's target, who is often a writer, public speaker, or blogger who does not have competent legal counsel (or who cannot afford such counsel) and who would rather capitualte than be dragged through the costly and time-consuming legal process, all the while being publicly labeled as an intolerant Islamophobe. Second, such lawsuits serve as warning shots across the bow to other speakers and writers, who then engage in a form of self-censorship rather than risk being sued, regardless of whether the lawsuit has any merit.[3]

AFLC has encountered such tactics, and the proper response is to hire competent counsel (or have AFLC provide the counsel *pro bono*) and take the challenge head on. As just one example, a former "Multicultural Relations" officer at the Ohio Department of Homeland Security (OHS), who was terminated for falsifying his background and for lying about being fired from an earlier teaching position at a community college for improper sexual relations with a female student, filed a defamation lawsuit against several national security experts. In the lawsuit, Omar Alomari claimed that counter-terrorism experts Stephen Coughlin, John Guandolo, Patrick Poole, and Todd Sheets had defamed him by exposing his role as a former high-ranking official in the Jordanian government and his ties to terrorist

---

[3] CAIR initiated its defamation lawfare with two separate lawsuits. The first lawsuit was against Congressman Cass Ballenger for stating publicly that CAIR was a fundraising arm of Hezbollah. Council on Am. Islamic Rels., Inc. v. Ballenger, 366 F. Supp. 2d 28 (D.D.C. 2005) (dismissing the lawsuit on the grounds that the Congressman was immune from suit as a government employee speaking on matters of legislative concern). CAIR filed its second initiating lawsuit against Andy Whitehead, a Navy veteran who created a website called anti-CAIR that identified CAIR as a terrorist organization. After Whitehead's counsel demanded during discovery that CAIR disclose its fundraising sources and connection to Hamas and the Muslim Brotherhood, the parties entered into a confidential settlement agreement that did not require Whitehead to apologize or retract his statement. The lawsuit, however, came at an enormous legal cost to Whitehead. *See, e.g.*, Whitehead's description of the lawsuit at http://www.anti-cair-net.org/Dismissed and Dr. Daniel Pipe's excellent analysis of CAIR's use of lawfare to silence its critics at http://www.danielpipes.org/1705/why-is-cair-suing-anti-cair.

organizations. AFLC represented the counter-terrorism experts in this litigation.

Alomari, a Muslim who emigrated from Jordan in 1978, claimed that the experts cast him in a "false light" by publishing allegedly false statements about him and, as a result of these statements, the OHS fired him. However, a federal court determined that the OHS terminated Alomari because he lied about his prior relationships to undisclosed organizations on his OHS application for employment and he lied about the fact that he lost his teaching position at Columbus State Community College as a result of an inappropriate sexual relationship with one of his female students.

In his lawsuit, Alomari alleged that the counter-terrorism experts had defamed him during counter-terrorism workshops and training sessions conducted for the Columbus, Ohio, police department by exposing Alomari's nefarious ties to terrorists. Alomari also alleged that Patrick Poole had published articles linking him to terrorists.

Alomari dismissed his lawsuit in response to a demand letter sent on behalf of the counter-terrorism experts by AFLC attorney David Yerushalmi. In his letter, Yerushalmi accused Alomari and his attorney of filing meritless and frivolous claims, and he gave them an ultimatum: either dismiss the frivolous claims immediately or face a motion for sanctions. Alomari chose the former, and his dismissal was with prejudice, ending this litigation.

In sum, this is lawfare doctrine: use and abuse the legal system to frighten anyone who might stand up to the Muslim Brotherhood and its ongoing effort to insinuate operatives into sensitive government positions. This case demonstrates that when you confront Islamist lawfare with better and even more aggressive lawyering, the truth and the Constitution are most often the victors.[4]

---

[4] Another example of CAIR surrogates using defamation to silence critics of the Muslim Brotherhood was a CAIR-associated lawyer's $10,000,000 defamation lawsuit against anti-jihad blogger Pamela Geller. The plaintiff, Omar Tarazi, who had worked for CAIR-Ohio, was retained to represent the parents of Rifqa Barry, the young teenage girl who converted to Christianity only to have her father threaten her with death—the classic honor killing prevalent in Muslim societies. Tarazi and CAIR decided to target Geller with a monstrous defamation lawsuit in Ohio alleging that her allegation that Tarazi was connected to the terrorist organization CAIR, was false. AFLC represented Geller *pro bono* and after more than a year of hard-fought discovery, forced Tarazi to dismiss his lawsuit or face the prospects of an adverse judicial ruling based on the defense of truth. *See* AFLC's

Abuse of Legal Process

Another lawfare tactic of the Muslim Brotherhood is to abuse the legal process to silence speech and to strike fear into those who might publicly oppose its agenda. A classic example of this form of lawfare occurred recently in a small town in Michigan. In fact, this example demonstrates another tactic employed by the Muslim Brotherhood: using federal civil rights statutes in an offensive posture.

In 2012, the Muslim Community Association of Ann Arbor (MCA) requested that Pittsfield Township rezone a parcel of land to build an Islamic School and community center.[5] The township denied the request, citing infrastructure and traffic concerns. Nevertheless, CAIR filed a federal civil rights lawsuit against the township on behalf of the MCA, alleging that township officials denied the MCA's rezoning application out of discrimination against Muslims. CAIR advanced constitutional claims and also invoked the Religious Land Use and Institutionalized Persons Act (RLUIPA), a federal statute that prohibits local governments from discriminating in its zoning decisions on the basis of religion.[6]

---

description of the litigation at http://www.americanfreedomlawcenter.org/case/tarazi-v-geller/.

5 It is not surprising that the Muslim Brotherhood is bent on constructing as many mosques as possible within the local communities. A leading international peer-reviewed journal specializing in the empirical study of terrorism has published a study that found that 80% of U.S. mosques provide their worshippers with jihad-style literature promoting the use of violence against non-believers and that the imams in those mosques expressly promote that literature. The study, which was co-authored by David Yerushalmi, also found that when a mosque imam or its worshippers were "Shariah-adherent," as measured by certain behaviors in conformity with Islamic law, the mosque was more likely to provide this violent literature and the imam was more likely to promote it. The study may be accessed at Perspectives on Terrorism: http://www.terrorismanalysts.com/pt/index.php/pot/article/view/sharia-adherence-mosque-survey. A copy is enclosed in the appendix. Moreover, any opposition to the construction of a mosque is promptly met with a RLUIPA lawsuit, see infra, and local government officials, who are often operating on a tight budget, know it and are therefore often unwilling to incur the costs required to resist the Muslim Brotherhood's efforts.

6 RLUIPA generally forbids any government from imposing a "substantial burden" on religious uses of land unless those restrictions are necessary to further a compelling government interest.   42 U.S.C. § 2000cc(a)(1) ("No government shall impose or implement a land use regulation in a manner that imposes a substantial burden on the

The MCA's rezoning request was opposed by a group of township residents who live in the neighborhood of the proposed development. The residents expressed concerns about the traffic congestion that would be caused by the construction of the school and community center. Pursuant to their rights protected by the First Amendment, these private citizens circulated and submitted to their elected township officials a petition expressing their opposition to the rezoning and several of them spoke out at public hearings held by the township to discuss the matter.

As a result of the citizens' involvement, CAIR served harassing subpoenas on a number of these citizens, demanding that they produce private emails and other documents, and in some cases, appear for a deposition. In one instance, a township resident, Ms. Zaba Davis, and her husband came home to find several papers jammed in the crack of the front door of their home. The papers included subpoenas demanding the production of personal emails and other documents and a subpoena commanding Ms. Davis to appear at a deposition.

In response to CAIR's abusive discovery requests, AFLC, which is representing seven of the targeted private citizens, filed a motion to "quash" and for a protective order against CAIR. The federal court granted the motion, ruling that the subpoenas violated the First Amendment and caused undue burden, and took the unusual step of sanctioning CAIR, ordering it to pay $9,000 in legal fees to AFLC. According to the court's ruling:

[CAIR] contends that its sole interest in deposing Davis stems from a genuine belief that she has what it believes to be relevant information, and not from any personal malice against her for her public opposition to the school. This argument fails for a few reasons. First, the Court finds unpersuasive [CAIR's] relevance argument. Second, for the reasons noted in the preceding paragraphs, to the extent information possessed by Davis is relevant, that relevance is far outweighed by the chilling effect that allowing the subpoenas would have on speech, not only for Davis, but for all others who wish to be involved in public discourse on matters of public concern.[7]

In sum, private citizens have a fundamental First Amendment right to publicly express to their elected officials their personal views.

---

religious exercise of a person, including a religious assembly or institution," unless such a regulation is necessary in furtherance of a compelling state interest.).

[7] A copy of the full ruling of the court is enclosed in the appendix.

CAIR's ruthless attacks demonstrate that its objectives are dangerously at odds with the Constitution. Consequently, this ruling was important not only for the individuals directly involved, but for all private citizens who want to speak out against the Muslim Brotherhood's agenda without fear of retribution. This case is a prime example of CAIR attempting to abuse the legal system to persecute its enemies, but AFLC stood in its way. Moreover, by sanctioning CAIR and awarding AFLC its attorneys' fees, this ruling is not only a victory against civilization jihad, but it is a victory with a stick, which is important in this battle.

In 2015, CAIR filed a federal civil rights lawsuit against TEOTWAWKI Investments, LLC, the company that owns and operates Florida Gun Supply, because its owner declared his retail gun supply store a "Mulsim Free Zone" following the Chattanooga, Tennessee terrorist attack in which five servicemembers were gunned down. The owner of the gun store refuses to equip the next Fort Hood, Chatanooga, or Garland, Texas terrorist with dangerous firearms. Pursuant to its official, written policy, Florida Gun Supply "will not serve: (a) Anyone who is either directly or indirectly associated with terrorism in any way; (b) Anyone associated in any way with an organization that is associated with terrorism; (c) Anyone who causes, or seeks to cause, any disturbance whatsoever at the limited liability company; (d) Anyone who is not permitted to purchase or possess a firearm under any federal, State, or local law or guideline; (e) Anyone who seeks to do harm to the interests of the United States; (f) Any person, in the sole judgment of the limited liability company, its owners, managers, and employees, who may pose a threat to public safety based on the person's behavior, comments, history, dress, or other such factors indicating that the person may be a threat to public safety. This judgment will not be based solely upon a person's race, color, religion, or sex."

Consistent with his legitimate concerns about public safety, the owner of Florida Gun Supply refused to meet with and train the Chief Executive Director for CAIR-Florida, citing the fact that CAIR was an unindicted co-conspirator in the largest terrorism financing trial prosecuted to date by the federal government, the fact that the United Arab Emirates has declared CAIR a terrorist organization, and the fact that the FBI has severed its ties with CAIR because of the organization's terrorist connections.

Nonetheless, CAIR-Florida sued Florida Gun Supply, allegeing religious discrimination under Title II of the Civil Rights Act. CAIR-

Florida claims that it is being unlawfully denied the "full and equal enjoyment of the goods, services, facilities, privileges, advantages, and accommodations of [a] place of public accommodation" on the basis of religioin. Of couse, this claim is false. AFLC is representing Florida Gun Supply in this federal lawsuit, which was filed in the U.S. District Court for the Southern District of Florida. AFLC has filed a motion requesting that the court dismiss the case.

In addition to Florida Gun Supply, AFLC is representing Second Amemendment gun rights advocate Jan Morgan and her business, The Gun Cave, because CAIR has requested that the Department of Justice investigate Ms. Morgan and her business because she too has publicly stated that she will not train Islamic terrorists at her gun range, which is located in Arkansas. No formal legal action has been taken as of yet against Ms. Morgan or The Gun Cave.

Enforcement of Shariah in American Courts

While often met with skepticism, the claim that shariah is being enforced in America's courts is verifiably true. A classic example of a state court enforcing shariah is the case of *Hosain v. Malik.*[8] Here, a Maryland appellate court agreed with a lower court's decision to defer to the Pakistan Shariah Court, which granted sole, unrestricted custody of a child to her father even though the mother was not provided due process in the proceedings. The mother had argued that if she had gone to Pakistan to contest the case, she would have been subject to capital punishment for having a new relationship with a man not sanctioned by shariah. Nonetheless, the Maryland appellate court ruled that her failure to go to Pakistan and face the risk of execution precluded her from making a public policy argument against the enforcement of shariah.

In this case, a public policy initiative of CSP and AFLC known as American Laws for American Courts (ALAC) would have provided the Maryland appellate court the legislative clarity to reverse the lower court's decision.

ALAC is model legislation that precludes state courts from giving effect to foreign laws or foreign judgments when the application of those foreign laws or foreign judgments would deprive a party in the proceeding of a constitutional right or liberty. The operative language of ALAC

---

[8] *Hosain v. Malik*, 108 Md. App. 284, 287 (Md. Ct. Spec. App. 1996).

provides that the foreign law is unenforceable only if its application to the litigation at hand would actually or foreseeably deny a party's constitutional rights. In other words, a state court might very well apply shariah or the law of England, as courts do all of the time in the appropriate circumstance (for example, the parties agree to such laws in a contract), as long as the particular aspect of shariah or the law of England applied in the "matter at issue" does not undermine our own state and federal constitutions. ALAC is agnostic about whether the foreign law is a religious law or a secular foreign law.[9]

Opponents of ALAC—the most vocal being CAIR—typically mischaracterize ALAC in an effort to drag it into a dispute with Jewish law and Catholic canon law, presumably to enlist Jewish and Catholic opponents to ALAC. But there is literally no instance of Jewish law or Catholic canon law being applied in a state court where a litigant is likely to be deprived of a constitutional liberty. And the reason this is so is because neither of these religious laws occupy the space of authoritative state law. Shariah is problematic precisely because it is the secular law in almost all of the Muslim world, either as the law of the land simply or as the authoritative law in matters of family relations and citizenship, or what is sometimes referred to as "identity law" in those Muslim countries which require their citizens to declare a religious affiliation for their "identity" cards—such that the law treats Muslim citizens differently from non-Muslims. Moreover, U.S. constitutional law already prohibits any state or federal law from infringing on what the courts have determined to be legitimate applications of religious freedom.[10]

Thus, if a church dispute erupts and lands in a state court, the abstention doctrine announced by our Supreme Court precludes a state court from intervening unless that intervention is based on a dispute that can be resolved on wholly secular, religiously-neutral grounds. In other words, religious arbitral bodies are constitutionally protected when they apply religious laws to purely ecclesiastical disputes and ALAC may not, as a matter of First Amendment law, apply. *See, e.g., supra* n.8.

The next type of attack on ALAC is not actually a criticism of ALAC *per se*, but a poorly constructed argument that ALAC is not

---

[9] A copy of this model legislation is enclosed in the appendix at __.

[10] *See, e.g., Hosanna-Tabor Evangelical Lutheran Church & Sch. v. EEOC,* 132 S. Ct. 694, 695 (2012) (recognizing that the ministerial exception, grounded in the First Amendment, precluded application of employment discrimination legislation to claims concerning the employment relationship between a religious institution and its ministers).

necessary. And this argument typically begins by assaulting the presumed motivations of the law as "anti-Muslim." This attack is sometimes presented in more nuanced form by trying to argue that shariah is not what it is throughout the Muslim world: that is, a religious/political/military body of law that requires death or beatings for blasphemy (so no freedom of speech) and apostasy (so no freedom of religion) and which demands a world ruled by Muslims pursuant to shariah. This argument then asserts that the illicit motive of ALAC is the "fear of creeping shariah." Well, yes and no.

ALAC understands there is a growing problem in state and federal courts of transnationalism, or the globalization of both politics and law. In other words, ALAC is a legitimate protection of the U.S. Constitution and prohibits foreign law and foreign judgments from usurping our constitutionally guaranteed liberties—a principle goal of civilization jihad.

Indeed, ALAC's critics are either not aware of, or purposefully avoid the SPEECH Act, which was passed by Congress and signed by the President in 2010.[11] The SPEECH Act was in reality a kind of federal ALAC, but limited to the First Amendment and free speech rights. It was necessitated by the fact that authors, researchers, and publishers who published facts about the financing and sponsoring of jihad from the golden tents of Saudi Arabia, Qatar, and Dubai, would find that they had been sued in England where the libel laws are so liberal they permit the suppression of free speech that would never pass muster in the United States. Indeed, this too was another form of civilization jihad. Once the offended plaintiff obtained a judgment in England, he would travel to the United States and find a state court to grant the judgment comity, turning the plaintiff into a judgment creditor who could now use the police power of the state to have the sheriff physically enforce the judgment.

The practice was so prevalent and dangerous it became known as "libel tourism." In response, Congress passed the SPEECH Act, which, like ALAC, prohibited granting those judgments comity if they did not provide the protections of our own First Amendment. And why was this necessary? Because state courts were not sure how to deal with this problem of transnationalism, which itself is a form of civilization jihad.

---

[11] Securing the Protection of our Enduring and Established Constitutional Heritage (SPEECH) Act, Pub. L. No. 111-223, 124 Stat. 2480.

While all state courts have adopted the common law doctrine of "void as against public policy"—a doctrine which allows a court to ignore a foreign law or judgment that might otherwise be given effect if that foreign law is repugnant to the public policy of the state—courts were not sure what the public policy was or should be. And this lack of clarity was built into the "void as against public policy doctrine" because courts did not want to be in the business of legislating public policy limits. In every state you can find appellate court decisions making clear that the state legislature must define the parameters of what the state public policy is. Thus, courts should only tepidly step into this arena.

ALAC takes up this judicial invitation to have the legislature make clear that any foreign law, religious or secular, that violates a party's constitutional liberties is void as a matter of public policy.

ALAC critics typically attempt to make this point of "not necessary" by claiming that the few well-known cases they know about, such as the trial judge in New Jersey who held that a woman could not obtain a restraining order preventing her husband from raping her because the man was simply following his "cultural norms" (*i.e.*, shariah), have been overturned on appeal. But this ignores the Maryland appellate court decision discussed above and the study published by CSP that tracked 146 cases of this sort.[12] Any lawyer will tell you that if there are 146 published opinions from the appellate courts, there will be thousands of cases just like the New Jersey case where the judge applied shariah over U.S. law that are never published or appealed because the losing party simply didn't have the wherewithal to fight the court's ruling.

Versions of ALAC have already passed in Tennessee, Louisiana, Arizona, Kansas, Oklahoma, North Carolina, Washington and Alabama and legislatures in several other states are considering it. (Florida also enacted in 2014 a version of this legislation). The earliest of these laws have been on the books now for several years and have not even been challenged much less overturned. And the reason is simple: they are constitutional and good policy as well. In short, ALAC is a form of legislative lawfare that is critically necessary in this fight against civilization jihad.

---

[12] *See* the CSP study at http://www.centerforsecuritypolicy.org/wp-content/uploads/2014/12/Shariah_in_American_Courts1.pdf and a fuller presentation of the context of the study at http://www.centerforsecuritypolicy.org/2015/01/05/shariah-in-american-courts-the-expanding-incursion-of-islamic-law-in-the-u-s-legal-system/.

Complicit Government Officials

A pernicious form of civilization jihad involves situations where government officials are denying the constitutional rights of private citizens and thus effectively doing the bidding of the jihadist, whether wittingly or unwittingly, through the exercise of the government's police powers.

One of the most egregious examples of this occurred at an Arab festival held in Dearborn, Michigan in 2012, and it resulted in a civil rights lawsuit. The case, *Bible Believers v. Wayne County*, was brought by AFLC on behalf of several Christian evangelists who were violently attacked by a hostile Muslim mob while preaching at the Arab festival. Video of the assault went viral on YouTube.[13]

The lawsuit was filed in September 2012 on behalf of the Christians against Wayne County, the Wayne County Sheriff, and two Wayne County Deputy Chiefs for not only refusing to protect the Christians from the attack but also for threatening to arrest the Christians for disorderly conduct if they did not halt their free speech activity and immediately leave the festival area.

In 2013, a Michigan federal judge dismissed the lawsuit. In his ruling, the judge stated that "the actual demonstration of violence here provided the requisite justification for [the Wayne County sheriffs'] intervention, even if the officials acted as they did because of the effect the speech had on the crowd."[14] Pause for a moment and consider the implications of this ruling. The federal judge is saying that Muslim violence trumps the free speech rights of Christians. This not only turns the First Amendment on its head, but it creates perverse incentives for the violent "hecklers" and for law enforcement officials who might disagree with the speakers.

On August 27, a divided, three-judge panel of the U.S. Court of Appeals for the Sixth Circuit affirmed the dismissal of the lawsuit, finding that the violent response of the Muslim attackers justified the Wayne County sheriffs' order to the Christians to depart the festival area under threat of arrest for disorderly conduct.[15]

Circuit Judge Clay wrote a scathing dissent, stating, "The majority's first error is its conclusion that the First Amendment did not

---

[13] *See* https://www.youtube.com/watch?v=dBaTVwIJH-E&feature=player_embedded.

[14] *Bible Believers v. Wayne Cnty.*, 2013 U.S. Dist. LEXIS 68042, at *31 (E.D. Mich. May 14, 2013).

[15] Bible Believers v. Wayne County, 765 F.3d 578 (6th Cir. 2014).

protect [the Christians'] speech. This is not only wrong, it is dangerously wrong."[16] Tacitly acknowledging the civilization jihad implications of the case, Judge Clay further stated that "the First Amendment strongly counsels that we should not allow the state to criminalize speech on the grounds that it is *blasphemous*—even so blasphemous that the average adherent to the offended religion would react with violence."[17]

Within days of receiving the adverse ruling, AFLC filed a petition for rehearing en banc, requesting full court review. On October 23, the court granted the petition, which is a rarity. As noted by the Sixth Circuit's rules: "A petition for rehearing en banc is an *extraordinary procedure* intended to bring to the attention of the entire court *a precedent-setting error of exceptional public importance*." The three-judge panel decision is now vacated, and the case will be reheard by the entire court (15 active circuit court judges). Oral argument was heard by the en banc court on March 4, 2015, at the Sixth Circuit courthouse in Cincinnati, Ohio. As of this article's publication, we await the federal appellate court's ruling.

Other types of cases where offensive lawfare is effectively used against civilization jihad involve situations where government officials have attempted to censor speech critical of Islam and jihad. These cases typically involve requests by private citizens to display advertisements on government transit authority property which then raise First Amendment issues because it is the government that is acting as the speech regulator. When the request is denied, a federal civil rights lawsuit is filed. AFLC has been involved in many such lawsuits brought on behalf of the American Freedom Defense Initiative (AFDI) and its directors, Pamela Geller and Robert Spencer. Here are several important examples.

In 2011, the New York Metropolitan Transit Authority (MTA) rejected an advertisement proposed by AFDI that stated, "In any war between the civilized man and the savage, support the civilized man. Support Israel. Defeat jihad." AFDI's anti-jihad message was submitted as a direct response to a pro-Palestine / anti-Israel advertisement that the MTA ran previously. The anti-Israeli advertisement suggested that Israel's military is the impediment to peace between the Israelis and Palestinians and that U.S. military aid to Israel also acts as an impediment to peace. In other words, the anti-Israel advertisement blames Israel, its military, and U.S. military aid to Israel as the cause of Palestinian terror directed against

---

[16] *Id.* at 596 (Clay, J., dissenting).
[17] *Id.* at 598 (Clay, J., dissenting).

innocent civilians in Israel and abroad. In short, the ad was an effort to influence public policy to advantage the jihadists.

AFDI's advertisement, on the other hand, presented the message that there is no comparison or equivalence between savage civilian-targeting violence and Israel's civilized struggle for survival in a part of the world where civilized behavior is overshadowed by terrorism and despotism.

AFLC's attorneys filed a civil rights lawsuit in federal court in New York City and won.[18] The judge ordered the MTA to display AFDI's advertisement and pay attorneys' fees, an amount in excess of one hundred twenty-eight thousand dollars. This decision was not only a victory for the right to freedom of speech, but it also prompted extensive media coverage, thereby providing a platform to educate the public about the threat of jihad abroad and here in the United States.

In 2012, when the Washington Metropolitan Area Transit Authority (WMATA) agreed to run a similar pro-Palestine / anti-Israel advertisement, AFDI submitted its anti-jihad message in response. WMATA rejected the anti-jihad advertisement, citing "world events" (*i.e.,* the September 2012 violent uprisings in the Middle-East caused by Muslims who claimed to be angered by a YouTube clip mocking the life of Muhammad) and concerns for the "security and safety" of its passengers.

AFLC promptly filed a civil rights lawsuit in the U.S. district court in Washington, D.C., and won.[19] The federal judge ordered WMATA to display the advertisement and pay attorneys' fees.[20]

In June 2013, King County, which provides public transportation in the Seattle, Washington area, displayed an advertisement submitted by the federal government that depicted the "Faces of Global Terrorism." The advertisement, which was an effort to "stop a terrorist" and "save lives," offered "up to $25 million reward" for helping to capture one of the

---

[18] *Am. Freedom Def. Initiative v. Metro. Transit Auth.*, 880 F. Supp. 2d 456 (S.D.N.Y. 2012).

[19] *Am. Freedom Def. Initiative v. Wash. Metro. Area Transit Auth.*, 898 F. Supp. 2d 73 (D.D.C. 2012).

[20] With the tragic murders committed by jihadist gunmen at the Paris office of *Charlie Hebdo*, defeating efforts by the government to censor speech because of fear of Muslim violence is critical. In short, an important goal of lawfare is to defeat efforts to silence speech due to threats of violence, threats which inevitably come from jihadists and others who want to suppress speech critical of Islam.

FBI's most wanted terrorists. This advertisement was part of the State Department's "Rewards for Justice" program.[21]

The terrorists identified in the advertisement are also found on the FBI's most wanted terrorist list, which is posted on the FBI's website.[22] At the time, this list included pictures and "wanted posters" for thirty-two terrorists. Of the thirty-two listed terrorists, thirty were individuals with Muslim names and/or are wanted for terrorism related to organizations conducting terrorist acts in the name of Islam.

Not long after the advertisement was displayed, politically correct politicians and Muslim advocacy groups complained because the list of wanted global terrorists pictured in the advertisement included mostly Muslim terrorists, which they found to be offensive. As a result of the complaints, the federal government terminated the advertisement campaign.

On July 30, 2013, Pamela Geller and Robert Spencer, who were appalled that the federal government caved into the complaints at the expense of American national security, submitted their own advertisement to King County on behalf of their organization, AFDI. This advertisement included the same pictures, names, and message as the government's advertisement.

Despite having previously accepted the federal government's "Faces of Global Terrorism" advertisement, on August 15, 2013, King County rejected AFDI's advertisement, claiming that it violated their advertising guidelines. Specifically, King Country claimed that the advertisement contained: (1) "[M]aterial that is or that the sponsor reasonably should have known is false, fraudulent, misleading, deceptive or would constitute a tort of defamation or invasion of privacy"; (2) "material that demeans or disparages an individual, group of individuals or entity"; and (3) "material that is so objectionable as to be reasonably foreseeable that it will result in harm to, disruption of or interference with the transportation system" in violation of the County's Transit Advertising Policy.

---

[21] *See* http://www.rewardsforjustice.net/.

[22] *See, e.g.,* http://www.fbi.gov/wanted/wanted_terrorists/@@wanted-group-listing (last visited Jan. 14, 2015) (currently listing thirty most wanted terrorists, twenty-eight of whom are individuals with Muslim names and/or are wanted for terrorists acts committed in the name of Islam).

As a result of King County's rejection of AFDI's advertisement, AFLC filed a federal civil rights lawsuit against the county. This case is still pending.

In September 2014, AFLC filed a federal civil rights lawsuit against the Southeastern Pennsylvania Transportation Authority (SEPTA) for refusing to run a "Stop the Islamic Jew-Hatred" advertisement. The lawsuit was filed in the U.S. district court in Philadelphia on behalf of the advertisement's sponsors, AFDI and its directors, Pamela Geller and Robert Spencer.

This case has a particularly interesting and unique twist. SEPTA claimed that it could ban the advertisement based on the argument that the message was false and thus not protected by the First Amendment. To support its argument, SEPTA intended to present the testimony of Dr. Jamal J. Elias, a professor at the University of Pennsylvania and "an eminent scholar of Islam and Muslim society" at a hearing on a motion for a preliminary injunction allegedly to establish the falsity of the advertisement. Dr. Elias intended to offer two opinions, both of which pertain to alleged inaccuracies in the advertisement. First, Dr. Elias intended to testify that referring to Haj Amin al-Husseini as the "leader of the Muslim word" is "manifestly false." And second, Dr. Elias intended to opine that the statement "the Qur'an teaches Jew-Hatred" is "unfair and erroneous." AFLC filed a motion requesting that the judge exclude the "expert" testimony because SEPTA's argument conflicted with the First Amendment. The judge agreed.[23]

In his ruling rejecting SEPTA's claim of "falsity," the judge reviewed relevant First Amendment precedent, observing that "speech concerning public issues has always rested on the highest rung of the hierarchy of First Amendment values. . . . As such, if there is any fixed star in our constitutional constellation, it is that no official, high or petty, can prescribe what shall be orthodox in politics, nationalism, religion, or other matters of opinion. Therefore, the protection afforded to political speech does not turn on the truth or popularity of the sentiments expressed."[24]

The judge further noted: "Long standing Supreme Court precedent instructs that political speech does not lose First Amendment protection simply because the listener believes that it is false or disagrees with the message it advances. Allowing the state to restrict political speech

---

[23] *Am. Freedom Def. Initiative v. Southeastern Pa. Transp. Auth.* ("SEPTA"), No. 2:14-5335, 2014 U.S. Dist. LEXIS 164575 (E.D. Pa. Nov. 25, 2014).

[24] *Id.* at *5.

based on an assessment that it is false or inaccurate, offends bedrock First Amendment principles."[25]

The judge concluded: "In light of the precedent discussed above, I find that First Amendment principles apply to the advertisement at issue regardless of its alleged falsity. Consequently, Dr. Elias' conclusions regarding the advertisement's veracity are not relevant and will be excluded from the preliminary injunction hearing."[26]

This was a significant victory for free speech, particularly in light of the fact that many government officials—this current administration being at the top of the list—often parrot the politically correct narrative that violent jihad does not represent "true" Islam. Indeed, it would be perilous to permit government censors to be the arbiter's of truth on matters such as religion and history.

While AFLC has achieved offensive lawfare victories by filing numerous lawsuits against government transit authorities across the country, on several occasions victory was achieved by merely threatening litigation.

For example, after the Chicago Transit Authority (CTA) refused to run advertisements countering CAIR's "my jihad" propaganda campaign—a campaign designed to change public opinion regarding the violent nature of jihad by claiming that the real meaning of "jihad" for Muslims includes such innocuous acts as staying fit—AFLC threatened the CTA with a lawsuit. CTA's general counsel promptly responded by reversing the CTA's decision and allowing the counter advertisements to run, citing AFLC's legal victories in New York and Washington, D.C., as the basis for the reversal.[27]

A Florida transit authority paid AFLC's clients not to sue and accepted AFLC's condition that it prohibit all non-commercial advertisements—thus preventing the display of CAIR advertisements that the proposed advertisements were meant to counter.

More recently, AFLC achieved another lawfare victory for free speech by forcing, under threat of litigation, the San Francisco Municipal Transportation Agency (SFMTA) to display an advertisement that exposes Islam's hatred of Jews and urges the U.S. government to stop all aid to Islamic countries. In addition, SFMTA, through its advertising agent

---

[25] *Id.* at *8.

[26] *Id.* at *10.

[27] *See* http://www.americanfreedomlawcenter.org/wp-content/uploads/2013/02/AFDI-Letter.pdf.

Titan, agreed to cover more than $10,000 of the associated advertising costs.

As the "Jew Hatred in the Quran" advertisement was going up in San Francisco, the public was watching the jihadist terror attack at the *Charlie Hebdo* office in Paris develop as hostages were taken at a Jewish deli on the eve of the Jewish Sabbath—the deli's busiest hours. This timing resulted in substantial media coverage, and it forced the uncomfortable discussions necessary in a free society for evaluating and re-evaluating public policy. Indeed, news agencies were forced to confront the reality of public discourse being driven by a simple advertisement. For example, in a local CBS newscast, the anchor asked the on-scene reporter if the San Francisco transit authority was planning on keeping these "truly controversial ads" on display. The reporter provided the government's answer: "The ads are staying up [because] if they did not keep these ads up, it almost certainly would end up in a lawsuit."[28] And in a local Fox report, the spokesman for the SFMTA stated, "We certainly understand that people might be offended by these ads . . . We have to run these ads because if we don't, it could result in a lawsuit that requires [SFMTA] to post them anyways. Then at the same time, we're using taxpayer dollars to pay for a lawsuit rather than improving service."[29] This is an example of the effective (and good) use of lawfare.

Other Offensive / Counter Lawfare Cases

In 2008, AFLC attorneys David Yerushalmi and Robert Muise filed the case of *Murray v. United States Department of Treasury*, which alleged that the U.S. government's takeover and financial bailout of AIG violated the Establishment Clause of the First Amendment.

At the time of the government bailout, which began in September 2008, AIG was the world leader in promoting shariah-compliant insurance products. As alleged in the lawsuit, by propping up AIG with taxpayer funds, the U.S. government was directly and indirectly promoting Islam—and, more troubling, shariah.

In May 2009, the Michigan federal judge presiding over the case rejected the Department of Justice's motion to dismiss the lawsuit, and later rebuffed efforts to stay the proceeding so the government could avoid

---

[28] See https://www.youtube.com/watch?v=wFNAWcCb-9g.

[29] *See* https://www.youtube.com/watch?v=v2Z0-G52V8M#t=113.

discovery and take an extraordinary appeal to the U.S. Court of Appeals for the Sixth Circuit. In that ruling, the judge stated:

In this case, the fact that AIG is largely a secular entity is not dispositive: The question in an as-applied challenge is not whether the entity is of a religious character, but how it spends its grant. The circumstances of this case are historic, and the pressure upon the government to navigate this financial crisis is unfathomable. Times of crisis, however, do not justify departure from the Constitution. In this case, the United States government has a majority interest in AIG. AIG utilizes consolidated financing whereby all funds flow through a single port to support all of its activities, including Sharia-compliant financing. Pursuant to the [Emergency Economic Stabilization Act], the government has injected AIG with tens of billions of dollars, without restricting or tracking how this considerable sum of money is spent. At least two of AIG's subsidiary companies practice Sharia-compliant financing, one of which was unveiled after the influx of government cash. . . . Finally, after the government acquired a majority interest in AIG and contributed substantial funds to AIG for operational purposes, the government co-sponsored a forum entitled "Islamic Finance 101." These facts, taken together, raise a question of whether the government's involvement with AIG has created the effect of promoting religion and sufficiently raise Plaintiff's claim beyond the speculative level, warranting dismissal inappropriate at this stage in the proceedings.[30]

After a year of document requests, depositions of current and former government witnesses, and three separate subpoenas issued to AIG and the New York Federal Reserve Bank, Yerushalmi and Muise filed a motion for summary judgment, arguing that the undisputed facts demonstrate that the government, through its absolute control and ownership of AIG, and with tens of billions of taxpayer dollars, has directly and indirectly promoted and supported shariah as a religious legal doctrine in violation of the U.S. Constitution.

A year's worth of discovery uncovered the following facts in addition to what was known from the public record:

- AIG had five wholly-owned subsidiaries which promote and practice shariah in Saudi Arabia, Malaysia, Bahrain, and the United States.

---

[30] *Murray v. Geithner*, 624 F. Supp. 2d 667, 676-77 (E.D. Mich. 2009).

- These shariah-compliant companies employed or otherwise retained the services of shariah authorities to tell them how to conduct their business according to shariah, including the shariah-compliant charities to which these AIG subsidiaries must contribute.

- The government placed absolutely no controls on how its billions were used by the shariah-compliant companies or to whom they supported with their "zakat" tax dollars. Moreover, these companies all accepted shariah's mandate to support jihad with zakat insofar as they abided by the authoritative rulings of the world's leading shariah authorities.

- Over one billion taxpayer dollars flowed through AIG's headquarters into supporting AIG's shariah businesses worldwide.

The government actively promoted shariah and shariah-compliant finance in many ways and venues:

- The Treasury Department published, edited, and updated articles about shariah-compliant finance, which essentially promote Islamic law uncritically.

- The Treasury Department created and staffed a position called the Islamic Finance Scholar-in Residence. No other religious law was so honored.

- Published presentations by senior Treasury Department officials lauded shariah-compliant finance and stated explicitly that the U.S. government "places significant importance on promoting . . . Islamic finance" and has "recently deepened our engagement in Islamic finance in a number of ways," including a "call[] for harmonization of Shari'a standards at the national and international levels."

- After the AIG bailout, the Treasury Department co-sponsored a half-day conference called "Islamic Finance 101" for government policy makers which was in effect a program to promote shariah and shariah-compliant finance.

It is one thing that the federal government felt compelled to bail out AIG after its fortunes were destroyed due to the company's own recklessness and bad acts. It is quite another thing to use U.S. taxpayer dollars to promote and support AIG's shariah businesses—all of which don't just sell shariah products to the Muslim world, but actively promote shariah as the best, most ethical way of life. Indeed, the shariah authorities relied upon by AIG's Shariah Supervisory Committees actively promoted jihad—and by jihad we mean kinetic war against the infidel West.

Consequently, through this litigation, AFLC's attorneys not only traced taxpayer money to support shariah, but found explicit public statements by senior Treasury officials actually telling the world that it is U.S. government policy to support shariah in the form of Islamic finance and even "call[ing] for harmonization of Shari'ah's standards."

Following the close of discovery, the Justice Department also filed a motion for summary judgment, arguing that the aid provided to AIG's shariah businesses was both unintended and *de minimus*.

On January 14, 2011, the judge completely reversed his earlier position and ruled that there was no evidence presented of religious indoctrination, and if there were such evidence, the indoctrination could not be attributed to the federal government. In addition, the court ruled that the amount of federal money that was used to support shariah—$153 million—was "*de minimus*" in light of the large sum of taxpayer money the federal government actually gave to AIG—in excess of $40 billion.[31] This ruling was immediately appealed to the Sixth Circuit, which unfortunately affirmed.[32]

While the case did not ultimately result in a favorable ruling, the ability to defeat a motion to dismiss and thus conduct extensive discovery proved invaluable in that AFLC was able to use this case to expose the federal government's endorsement of shariah-compliant financing, thereby forcing it to back away from its unchallenged support.

Finally, in a classic example of offensive lawfare aimed at a proponent of civilization jihad, AFLC is involved in litigation filed directly against CAIR. Five former clients of CAIR filed two separate lawsuits in federal court alleging common law and statutory fraud, breach of fiduciary duty, and intentional infliction of emotional distress. These two lawsuits followed an earlier lawsuit which had also alleged that CAIR's fraudulent conduct amounted to racketeering, a federal RICO crime.[33] In that case,

---

[31] *Murray v. Geithner*, 763 F. Supp. 2d 860 (E.D. Mich. 2011).

[32] *Murray v. United States Dep't of Treasury*, 681 F.3d 744 (6th Cir. 2012).

[33] The Racketeer Influenced and Corrupt Organizations Act (RICO), 18 U. S. C. §§ 1961-1968.

the court dismissed the RICO counts concluding that CAIR's conduct as alleged was fraudulent but not a technical violation of RICO.

The two remaining civil complaints were filed in the U.S. district court in Washington, D.C. in January 2010. Both lawsuits arose out of the same facts as the RICO lawsuit but based upon state law fraud claims. As a result, the court consolidated the two cases.

The lawsuits allege that Morris Days, the "Resident Attorney" and "Manager for Civil Rights" at the now defunct CAIR-MD/VA chapter in Herndon, Virginia, was in fact not an attorney and that he failed to provide legal services for clients who came to CAIR for legal representation. As alleged, CAIR knew of this fraud and purposefully conspired with Days to keep the CAIR clients from discovering that their legal matters were being mishandled or not handled at all.

While AFLC attorneys David Yerushalmi and Robert Muise represent the five plaintiffs in these two lawsuits, three of whom are Muslim Americans, the complaints allege that according to CAIR internal documents, there were hundreds of victims of the CAIR fraud scheme.

According to the complaints, CAIR knew or should have known that Days was not a lawyer when it hired him. But, like many organizations accused of wrongdoing, things got worse when CAIR officials were confronted with clear evidence of Days' fraudulent conduct. Rather than come clean and attempt to rectify past wrongs, CAIR conspired with Days to conceal and further the fraud.

To this end, CAIR officials purposefully concealed the truth about Days from their clients, law enforcement, the Virginia and D.C. state bar associations, and the media. When CAIR did get irate calls from clients about Days' failure to provide competent legal services, CAIR fraudulently deceived its clients about Days' relationship to CAIR, suggesting he was never actually employed by CAIR, and even concealing the fact that CAIR had fired him once some of the victims began threatening to sue.

According to the facts laid out in both complaints, CAIR has engaged in a massive criminal fraud in which literally hundreds of CAIR clients have been victimized and because of the CAIR cover-up they still don't realize it. The fact that CAIR has victimized Muslims and non-Muslims alike demonstrates that CAIR is only looking out for CAIR and its ongoing effort to bilk donors out of millions of dollars of charitable donations thinking they are supporting a legitimate civil liberties organization.

The complaints also allege that in addition to covering up the fraud scheme, CAIR forced angry clients who were demanding a return of their legal fees to sign a release that bought the client-victims' silence by prohibiting them from informing law enforcement or the media about the fraud. According to the agreement, if the "settling" clients said anything to anyone about the fraud scheme, CAIR would be able to sue them for $25,000.

This enforced code of silence left hundreds of CAIR's victims in the dark such that to this day they have not learned that Days was not an attorney and that he had not filed the legal actions on their behalf for which CAIR publicly claimed credit. Days has since died of a lung complication.

This case is still pending. In the interim, however, discovery in this case allowed AFLC's lawyers to uncover tax and money laundering violations by CAIR wherein CAIR received millions of dollars from their Brotherhood financiers from the oil-rich Gulf states such as Qatar, in effect acting as agents for a foreign sovereign, without properly disclosing the source of its funds or declaring its activities as a foreign agent.[34]

---

[34] *See* AFLC's description of CAIR's money laundering criminal operation at http://www.americanfreedomlawcenter.org/2013/09/20/council-on-american-islamic-relations-cair-the-largest-muslim-brotherhood-hamas-front-group-in-america/.

CONCLUSION

Lawfare is a potent weapon in the public policy battle against civilization jihad. However, it is also a weapon that is often employed by jihadists and their complicit associates to promote their illicit policy goals. Consequently, it is imperative that any serious strategy designed to oppose the Muslim Brotherhood's efforts to "sabotage" America "from within" include an aggressive and competent counter legal force to engage in offensive and defensive lawfare in this battlespace.

APPENDIX I: MUSLIM COMMUNITY ASSOCIATION OF ANN ARBOR V. PITTSFIELD TOWNSHIP, ET AL.

UNITED STATES DISTRICT COURT
EASTERN DISTRICT OF MICHIGAN
SOUTHERN DIVISION

MUSLIM COMMUNITY
ASSOCIATION OF ANN ARBOR,

                 Plaintiff,   Civil Action No. 12-cv-10803
                                           Honorable Patrick J. Duggan
                                           Magistrate Judge David R. Grand

v.

PITTSFIELD TOWNSHIP, *et al.*,

                 Defendants.

_____/

ORDER GRANTING NON-PARTY ZABA DAVIS' MOTION TO QUASH AND FOR PROTECTIVE ORDER [89]

Before the Court is Non-Party Zaba Davis' ("Davis") Motion to Quash and for Protective Order, filed on April 15, 2014. (Doc. #89). Defendant Muslim Community Association of Ann Arbor, d/b/a Michigan Islamic Academy, filed a response to this motion on May 2, 2014 (Doc. #94), and Davis filed a reply on May 9, 2014. (Doc. #101).[1] An Order of Reference was entered on April 16, 2014, referring this motion to the undersigned for determination. (Doc. #90). The Court dispenses with oral argument on this motion pursuant to E.D. Mich. L.R. 7.1(f).

I.   **Background**

Plaintiff Muslim Community Association of Ann Arbor is a non-profit corporation that does business as the Michigan Islamic Academy, an Islamic school offering secular and non-

---

[1] MCA's response brief was filed under seal, and it has refused Ms. Davis' request for unredacted copies of any sealed materials. The Court has reviewed the redacted documents supplied under seal and is perplexed and troubled that they were filed in that manner. However, because the Court is granting Davis' instant motion the issue of her access to such materials is moot. The Court also notes that no other party has raised a concern about the sealed materials.

secular curricula.[2] Apparently in 2010, the MCA sought to establish a new school building in the greater Ann Arbor community. *Id.* at 5-6. The proposed location for the new school fell within the zoning jurisdiction of Defendant Pittsfield Township. The Pittsfield Township Board of Trustees ("Board") is the body with ultimate authority to approve or deny zoning requests in that township. *Id.* at 14. However, the first step in the process is to go through the Pittsfield Township Planning Commission ("Planning Commission"), which screens zoning proposals and makes recommendations upon them.

In 2010, MCA began the process of purchasing property and seeking approval from Pittsfield Township to build a new school. *Id.* at 8. MCA contends that significant alterations to the original proposed site plan were effectuated in order to assuage concerns raised by the Planning Commission, and that traffic impact studies indicated that the school would not dramatically disrupt nearby roadways and intersections. *Id.* at 10. MCA further argues that it was subjected to an unusually onerous screening process. The Defendants disagree.

During public hearings about the proposed construction taking place during 2011, some citizens voiced concerns that the plan would lead to decreased property values and an increase in congestion. *Id.* at 11. Ultimately, the Planning Commission recommended to the Board that MCA's petition be denied on the grounds that it could lead to issues of traffic, noise, and visual screening. *Id.* at 13. The Board of Trustees unanimously adopted that recommendation on October 26, 2011, thus denying the construction petition. On February 22, 2012, MCA filed suit against Pittsfield Township and its Board of Trustees, alleging that the rejection of its petition to build a school was motivated, at least in part, by animus against the Islamic faith, and thus violated its due process rights. *Id.*

---

[2] For ease, the Court will simply refer to the Plaintiff and its d/b/a as the "MCA".

2

On April 1, 2014, MCA issued two subpoenas to non-party Zaba Davis, a community member who allegedly spoke out against the site plan.[3] (Doc. #89 at Ex. A, B). One subpoena commanded Davis to produce certain documents by April 16, 2014, while the other commanded her to appear for a deposition on April 17, 2014. (*Id.*) Specifically, the subpoena for production of documents required Davis to produce:

> A complete copy of any and all documents and correspondences (including the email header showing the sender, all recipients, date and time of such email), and all other communications with (1) Pittsfield Township or any representative of Pittsfield Township, including members of the Planning Department, Planning Commission and Board of Trustees, regarding the proposed Michigan Islamic Academy project (MIA); (2) Planning Commissioners Deborah Williams and Michael Yi regarding MIA; (3) neighboring residents regarding MIA. Include copies of all documents, correspondences, leaflets, petitions or other material or information on any medium created or distributed encouraging (1) neighboring residents to oppose MIA and to attend hearings before Pittsfield Township, and (2) Pittsfield Township representatives to oppose MIA.

(*Id.* at Ex. B).[4]

On April 15, 2014, Davis filed a motion to quash the subpoenas, arguing that they were not properly served on her, and that, substantively, the subpoenas represent an attempt to harass her for exercising her First Amendment right to express her views in opposition to the school's construction. (Doc. #89). In response, MCA argues that Deborah Williams, a member of the Planning Commission, testified at her deposition that Davis had been "enlisted by Commissioner Williams to cultivate [] opposition" to the proposed school, and that it "believes that the persons

---

[3] As discussed below, Davis contests the method of service of the subpoenas, claiming that they were shoved in her door on April 1, 2014. (Doc. #89 at 6).

[4] According to an affidavit of Davis' counsel, MCA also served identical subpoenas duces tecum on other individual neighbors of Davis. (Doc. #101 at Ex. 1, ¶ 2). Davis argues that although MCA apparently has abandoned its efforts to obtain documents from these other individuals, the mere fact that identical subpoenas were served on them suggests that the one directed to her was not narrowly tailored or "benign." (*Id.* at 4, fn. 2).

3

who distributed Commissioner Williams' leaflets purposefully avoided the homes of Muslim families, possibly at the behest of Commissioner Williams." (Doc. #94 at 9).[5]   Thus, MCA asserts, Davis may have information establishing or suggesting that Commissioner Williams voted to recommend denial of MCA's petition for discriminatory reasons.   MCA claims that it "is not interested in Ms. Davis. Rather, [it] is interested in the information she likely possesses about the efforts of and intentions behind Commissioner Williams' unprecedented, undisclosed, and successful campaign against Plaintiff's rezoning application." (*Id.* at 11).

II.   Legal Standard

The overall scope of allowable discovery is generally quite broad.   "Unless otherwise limited by a court order, the scope of discovery is as follows: Parties may obtain discovery regarding any nonprivileged matter that is relevant to any party's claim or defense." Fed. R. Civ. P. 26(b)(1).   Rule 45 of the Federal Rules of Civil Procedure authorizes a party to serve a subpoena on a non-party, and it is clear that such subpoenas are part of the "discovery" process contemplated by Rule 26.   *McGuire v. Warner*, 2009 WL 2370738, at *1 (E.D. Mich. Jul. 29, 2009) (citing cases).   Of course, the reach of discovery is not without restriction.   Rule 26 provides, "the court must limit the frequency or extent of discovery otherwise allowed by these rules … if it determines that… the burden or expense of the proposed discovery outweighs its likely benefit." Fed. R. Civ. P. 26(b)(2)(C).   Similarly, Rule 45 provides that, on a timely motion, "the court for the district where compliance is required must quash or modify a subpoena that: (i)

---

[5] However, Williams actually testified that Davis had said that she (Davis) would distribute a communication that Williams had written, but that Williams was unaware what, if anything, Davis did in that regard. (Doc. #97 at 38). Williams also specifically testified, contrary to MCA's unsupported "belief," that she and Davis did not coordinate efforts to distribute the communication. (*Id.* at 39). Similarly, Davis has averred that she did not take action at Williams' behest, and did not "skip" any Muslim homes when she distributed petitions. (Doc. #101 at Ex. 2).

4

fails to allow a reasonable time to comply; (ii) requires a person to comply beyond the geographical limits specified in Rule 45(c); (iii) requires disclosure of privileged or other protected matter, if no exception or waiver applies; or (iv) subjects a person to undue burden." Fed. R. Civ. P. 45(d)(3)(A)(i-iv).

In passing on such a motion to quash, the Court must "weigh the likely relevance of the requested material to the investigation…of producing the material." *E.E.O.C. v. Ford Motor Credit Co.*, 26 F.3d 44, 47 (6th Cir. 1994). Courts have declined to enforce subpoenas that do not strike the proper balance. *See United States v. Gammo*, 428 F. Supp. 2d 705, 708 (E.D. Mich. 2006) (quoting *United States v. Theodore*, 479 F.2d 749, 754 (4th Cir.1973)) ("where it appears that the purpose of the summons is 'a rambling exploration' of a third party's files, it will not be enforced.").

The "nonparty seeking to quash a subpoena bears the burden of demonstrating that the discovery sought should not be permitted." *Great Lakes Transp. Holding, LLC v. Yellow Cab Serv. Corp. of Florida, Inc.*, 11-50655, 2011 WL 2533653 (E.D. Mich. June 27, 2011) (quoting *Hansen Beverage Co. v. Innovation Ventures, LLC*, No. 09–50630, 2009 WL 2351769, at *1 (E.D. Mich. Jul. 28, 2009)). For the reasons discussed below, the Court finds that Davis has met her burden.

III. **Analysis**

A. *Service of Subpoenas*

Davis first argues that she was not properly served with the subpoenas at issue, as "[j]amming subpoenas in a door of an unoccupied residence does not constitute effective service." (Doc. #89 at 11). In response, MCA asserts that Ms. Davis was properly served: it asserts that it initially attempted to serve subpoenas on Davis via First Class Mail and that, only

5

when her attorneys objected to this method (and refused to accept service on her behalf), did it hire a process server "to go to Ms. Davis' home, attempt to personally serve her, and then leave the subpoena in her door." (Doc. #94 at 12). MCA further asserts that "Rule 45 requires 'delivering a copy [of the subpoena] to the named person," and states that this has been done twice – once by mail, and once by leaving a copy at Davis' home. (*Id.* at 12-13).

Fed. R. Civ. P. 45(b)(1) provides that, "Serving a subpoena requires delivering a copy to the named person and, if the subpoena requires that person's attendance, tendering the fees for 1 day's attendance and the mileage allowed by law." The issue, then, is whether Rule 45(b)(1)'s provision that a subpoena be "delivered" to the named person requires that the subpoena be *personally* served. Some courts have required personal service for a subpoena. *See, e.g., Benford v. American Broadcasting Co., Inc.,* 98 F.R.D. 40 (D.Md. 1983); *In re: Johnson & Johnson,* 59 F.R.D. 174 (D.Del. 1973).

Other courts have allowed some degree of flexibility in accomplishing proper service, including by the use of certified mail, if the manner can be reasonably assumed to ensure receipt of the subpoena. *See Halawani v. Wolfenbarger,* No. 07–15483, 2008 WL 5188813, at *4 (E.D. Mich. Dec. 10, 2008) ("nothing in the language of Rule 45 suggests that in-hand, personal service is required to effectuate "delivery," or that service by certified mail is forbidden."); *Franklin v. State Farm Fire & Cas. Co.,* 09-10947, 2009 WL 3152993 (E.D. Mich. Sept. 30, 2009) ("The growing number of cases that have determined that Rule 45 does not require personal service have permitted service by certified mail").

These decisions are grounded in the fact that Rule 45 does not explicitly state that subpoenas must be delivered by physically presenting it to the recipient. At the same time, some courts have qualified this flexibility by allowing it only after the serving party has "diligently

6

43

attempted to effectuate personal service." *Franklin v. State Farm Fire & Cas. Co.*, 2009 WL 3152993, at *1–2 (E.D. Mich. Sept. 30, 2009). As a result, courts have found inadequate subpoena service attempts when the requesting party failed to make adequate efforts to personally serve a subpoena. *OceanFirst Bank v. Hartford Fire Ins. Co.*, 794 F. Supp. 2d 752, 755 (E.D. Mich. 2011) (holding that because requesting party provided no reliable evidence that the subpoena was sent to the recipient's real address, there was not diligent effort likely to result in actual delivery).

In this case, MCA asserts that it attempted to serve Davis in several ways before leaving copies of the subpoenas at her residence. MCA asserts that it relied on First Class Mail initially, then sought to serve Davis through her attorneys, and finally hired a process server to go to Davis' residence in an attempt to serve her in person. (Doc. #94 at 12-13). Given that MCA attempted to serve Davis on at least three separate occasions, using three separate methods, it would seem to meet the diligence requirement. However, even assuming that service was accomplished, the Court finds that the subpoenas should be quashed on other grounds for the reasons discussed below.

B.   *Relevance and Undue Burden of Subpoenas*

Davis argues that the subpoenas seek irrelevant information and are unduly burdensome to comply with. She claims her role was that of a private citizen expressing her views and signing a petition, not one of a government official with authority to cast a vote on MCA's application. (Doc. #89 at 7). Davis points to the document subpoena's breadth, as it requests all documents and correspondence between her and a wide range of entities and persons, including her neighbors. Lastly, Davis argues that failing to quash the subpoena would have a chilling effect on the exercise of free speech.

7

44

As noted above, "courts have incorporated relevance as a factor when determining motions to quash a subpoena." *AFMS LLC v. United Parcel Serv. Co.*, 2012 WL 3112000 (S.D. Cal. July 30, 2012). And, this Court agrees that nonparty subpoenas ought to "require a stronger showing of relevance than for simple party discovery." *Stamy v. Packer*, 138 F.R.D. 412, 419 (D.N.J. 1990). Here, Davis has the better argument as to the subpoenas' relevancy and burden; the subpoenas seek her private correspondence with her neighbors, as well as any correspondence she had with Pittsfield Township and its representatives (most notably its Planning Commission and Board members) regarding MCA and its proposed school. (Doc. #89 at Ex. B). But Davis, as a private citizen, had no formal role whatsoever to play in either the Planning Commission's recommendation or the Board's ultimate vote.

In her brief, Davis asserts that "Judge Duggan [in a prior opinion unrelated opinion] was quite explicit: the information that that Plaintiff seeks here regarding any alleged actions of Deborah Williams (let alone any actions related to Davis or her neighbors) is not relevant to Plaintiff's claims." (Emphasis in original). Doc. #101 at 3-4. That assertion goes a bit too far – Judge Duggan merely stated that he was "somewhat troubled" by MCA's focus on the Planning Commission, which does not have ultimate authority to deny or approve zoning applications. (Doc. #58 at 26 n.9). Judge Duggan's order does not mention Deborah Williams, nor does it contain a blanket statement barring any investigation into her actions. Thus, the order does not necessarily dictate the instant motion's resolution.

Nevertheless, Davis has shown that the logical nexus between herself and the alleged injury is far too removed for the type of invasive discovery requested of her. The Board of Trustees has the legal authority to approve or deny the zoning petition, and is merely *advised* by the Planning Commission. Williams, who is not even a defendant in this action, is but a single

8

45

member of the Planning Commission. Davis has no affiliation with either the Board or the Planning Commission, and is merely a private citizen who, at most is alleged to have distributed materials which resulted in increased public opposition to MCA's application.[6] For this reason alone, the subpoenas directed to Davis must be quashed.

C.   *First Amendment Issues*

The subpoenas directed to Davis should also be quashed as an undue burden on her First Amendment rights. Courts have a long history of vigorously protecting a wide range of First Amendment activities, including anonymous identities, membership rolls, and associational affiliations. *See, e.g., Highfields Capital Mgmt., L.P. v. Doe, 385 F. Supp. 2d 969 (N.D. Cal. 2005); Britt v. Superior Court, 574 P.2d 766 (1978); NAACP v. Alabama, 357 U.S. 449 (1958).* And there can be no question that the activity Davis is alleged to have engaged in (which MCA is not claiming was unlawful) is protected by the First Amendment. As the United States Supreme Court explained in *N.A.A.C.P. v. Claiborne Hardware Co.*, 458 U.S. 886, 913 (1982) (internal citations omitted):

> This Court has recognized that expression on public issues "has always rested on the highest rung of the hierarchy of First Amendment values." "[S]peech concerning public affairs is more than self-expression; it is the essence of self-government." There is a "profound national commitment" to the principle that "debate on public issues should be uninhibited, robust, and wide-open."

Under these indelible principles it is clear that permitting third-party discovery into a private citizen's lawful actions on a matter of public debate would clearly cause her and other individuals to be hesitant about becoming involved in the political process. Indeed protecting

---

[6] And, as noted above, *supra* at 3-4, fn. 5, MCA's proffer as to the nature and extent of her involvement is extremely flimsy. Clearly, Williams' testimony suggests she and Davis were not working closely together, and MCA makes no allegation that Davis or Williams bribed or otherwise coerced any person into voicing opposition to MCA's application. Indeed, MCA states that it does not suspect Davis engaged in any wrongdoing. (Doc. #95 at 6).

9

against such a chilling effect is one of the First Amendment's very purposes. *See, e.g., Australia/Eastern U.S.A. Shipping Conference v. United States,* 537 F. Supp. 807, 810 (D.D.C. 1982) ("[T]here is no doubt that the overwhelming weight of authority is to the effect that forced disclosure of first amendment activities creates a chilling effect which must be balanced against the interests in obtaining the information.").

MCA contends that its sole interest in deposing Davis stems from a genuine belief that she has what it believes to be relevant information, and not from any personal malice against her for her public opposition to the school. (Doc. #94 at 9). This argument fails for a few reasons. First, as discussed above, the Court finds unpersuasive MCA's relevance argument. Second, for the reasons noted in the preceding paragraphs, to the extent information possessed by Davis is relevant, that relevance is far outweighed by the chilling effect that allowing the subpoenas would have on speech, not only for Davis, but for all others who wish to be involved in public discourse on matters of public concern.

Thus, at least on the record before the Court as to Davis' limited activities which were at least twice removed from the ultimate decisionmakers, the Court concludes that any interest that would be served by requiring her to produce any of the requested materials[7] is outweighed by the infringement on her First Amendment rights that would result from such compulsion.

IV.   Conclusion

Having fully considered Davis' alleged involvement in the matter (including the fact that her communications have no bearing on whether the Board itself acted with a discriminatory intent), the need to protect Davis' First Amendment rights, and the availability of other evidence,

---

[7] The Court also notes that many of the questions put to Williams during her deposition focused on emails exchanged between she and Davis that the MCA already possesses. And, to the extent the subpoenas seek correspondence between Davis and other Township officials, the MCA has other avenues of obtaining those materials.

10

the Court finds that Davis has shown that the subpoenas impose an undue burden on her. Accordingly, her motion to quash the subpoenas and for a protective order (Doc. #89) will be granted.[8]

Accordingly, **IT IS ORDERED** that Non-Party Zaba Davis' Motion to Quash and for Protective Order [89] is **GRANTED**. Davis need not take any further action with respect to the subpoenas which MCA directed to her. **IT IS FURTHER ORDERED** that, consistent with the terms outlined in footnote 8 above, Davis may pursue recovery of the fees and costs she reasonably incurred in connection with the instant motion

Dated: July 2, 2014
Ann Arbor, Michigan

s/David R. Grand
DAVID R. GRAND
United States Magistrate Judge

NOTICE TO THE PARTIES REGARDING OBJECTIONS

The parties' attention is drawn to Fed. R. Civ. P. 72(a), which provides a period of fourteen (14) days from the date of receipt of a copy of this order within which to file objections for consideration by the district judge under 28 U.S. C. §636(b)(1).

---

[8] Davis requests reimbursement of the fees and costs she incurred in filing her instant motion pursuant to Rule 37(a)(5)(A), which provides, in pertinent part:

> If the motion [for protective order] is granted ... the court must, after giving an opportunity to be heard, require the party or deponent whose conduct necessitated the motion, the party or attorney advising that conduct, or both to pay the movant's reasonable expenses incurred in making the motion, including attorney's fees.

Accordingly, within 30 days of the date of this Order (or if objections are filed which are overruled, within 30 days thereafter), counsel for Davis and the MCA shall meet and confer to discuss an appropriate amount of such fees and costs to be paid to her by the MCA. In the event no agreement is reached, Davis may, within that same timeframe, submit a properly-supported petition to the Court for her reasonable fees and costs. MCA may have 14 days after the filing of any such petition to file a response thereto.

11

CERTIFICATE OF SERVICE

The undersigned certifies that the foregoing document was served upon counsel of record via email addresses the Court has on file.

s/Eddrey O. Butts
EDDREY O. BUTTS
Case Manager

Dated: July 2, 2014

12

APPENDIX II: AMERICAN LAWS FOR AMERICAN COURTS MODEL ACT[35]

AN ACT to protect rights and privileges granted under the United States or [State] Constitution.

BE IT ENACTED BY THE [GENERAL ASSEMBLY/LEGISLATURE] OF THE STATE OF [_____]:

The [general assembly/legislature] finds that it shall be the public policy of this state to protect its citizens from the application of foreign laws when the application of a foreign law will result in the violation of a right guaranteed by the constitution of this state or of the United States, including but not limited to due process, freedom of religion, speech, or press, and any right of privacy or marriage as specifically defined by the constitution of this state.

The [general assembly/state legislature] fully recognizes the right to contract freely under the laws of this state, and also recognizes that this right may be reasonably and rationally circumscribed pursuant to the state's interest to protect and promote rights and privileges granted under the United States or [State] Constitution, including but not limited to due process, freedom of religion, speech, or press, and any right of privacy or marriage as specifically defined by the constitution of this state.

[1] As used in this act, "foreign law, legal code, or system" means any law, legal code, or system of a jurisdiction outside of any state or territory of the United States, including, but not limited to, international organizations and tribunals, and applied by that jurisdiction's courts, administrative bodies, or other formal or informal tribunals. For the purposes of this act, foreign law shall not mean, nor shall it include, any laws of the Native American tribes in this state.

As used in this act, "court" means any court, board, administrative agency, or other adjudicative or enforcement authority of this State.

As used in this Act, "religious organization" means any church, seminary, synagogue, temple, mosque, religious order, religious

---

[35] http://publicpolicyalliance.org/legislation/model-alac-bill/

corporation, association, or society, whose identity is distinctive in terms of common religious creed, beliefs, doctrines, practices, or rituals, of any faith or denomination, including any organization qualifying as a church or religious organization under section 501(c)(3) or 501(d) of the United States Internal Revenue Code.

[2] Any court, arbitration, tribunal, or administrative agency ruling or decision shall violate the public policy of this State and be void and unenforceable if the court, arbitration, tribunal, or administrative agency bases its rulings or decisions in the matter at issue in whole or in part on any law, legal code or system that would not grant the parties affected by the ruling or decision the same fundamental liberties, rights, and privileges granted under the U.S. and [State] Constitutions, including but not limited to due process, freedom of religion, speech, or press, and any right of privacy or marriage as specifically defined by the constitution of this state.

[3] A contract or contractual provision (if severable) which provides for the choice of a law, legal code or system to govern some or all of the disputes between the parties adjudicated by a court of law or by an arbitration panel arising from the contract mutually agreed upon shall violate the public policy of this State and be void and unenforceable if the law, legal code or system chosen includes or incorporates any substantive or procedural law, as applied to the dispute at issue, that would not grant the parties the same fundamental liberties, rights, and privileges granted under the U.S. and [State] Constitutions, including but not limited to due process, freedom of religion, speech, or press, and any right of privacy or marriage as specifically defined by the constitution of this state.

[4]

> a. A contract or contractual provision (if severable) which provides for a jurisdiction for purposes of granting the courts or arbitration panels *in personam* jurisdiction over the parties to adjudicate any disputes between parties arising from the contract mutually agreed upon shall violate the public policy of this State and be void and unenforceable if the jurisdiction chosen includes any law, legal code or system, as applied to the dispute at issue, that would not grant the parties the same fundamental liberties, rights, and privileges granted under the U.S. and [State] Constitutions, including but not limited to due process, freedom of religion, speech, or press, and any

right of privacy or marriage as specifically defined by the constitution of this state.

b. If a resident of this state, subject to personal jurisdiction in this state, seeks to maintain litigation, arbitration, agency or similarly binding proceedings in this state and if the courts of this state find that granting a claim of forum non conveniens or a related claim violates or would likely violate the fundamental liberties, rights, and privileges granted under the U.S. and [State] Constitutions of the non-claimant in the foreign forum with respect to the matter in dispute, then it is the public policy of this state that the claim shall be denied.

[5] Without prejudice to any legal right, this act shall not apply to a corporation, partnership, limited liability company, business association, or other legal entity that contracts to subject itself to foreign law in a jurisdiction other than this state or the United States.

[6] No court or arbitrator shall interpret this Act to limit the right of any person to the free exercise of religion as guaranteed by the First Amendment to the U.S. Constitution and by the Constitution of this State. No court shall interpret this Act to require or authorize any court to adjudicate, or prohibit any religious organization from adjudicating, ecclesiastical matters, including, but not limited to, the election, appointment, calling, discipline, dismissal, removal or excommunication of a member, officer, official, priest, nun, monk, pastor, rabbi, imam or member of the clergy, of the religious organization, or determination or interpretation of the doctrine of the religious organization, where adjudication by a court would violate the prohibition of the establishment clause of the First Amendment of the United States, or violate the Constitution of this State.

[7] This statute shall not be interpreted by any court to conflict with any federal treaty or other international agreement to which the United States is a party to the extent that such treaty or international agreement preempts or is superior to state law on the matter at issue.

APPENDIX III: PERSPECTIVES ON TERRORISM: SHARIA ADHERENCE MOSQUE SURVEY

Also available at:

http://www.terrorismanalysts.com/pt/index.php/pot/article/view/sharia-adherence-mosque-survey/340

Sharia Adherence Mosque Survey: Correlations between *Sharia* Adherence and Violent Dogma in U.S. Mosques

by Dr. Mordechai Kedar and David Yerushalmi, Esq.

Abstract

A random survey of 100 representative mosques in the U.S. was conducted to measure the correlation between Sharia adherence and dogma calling for violence against non-believers. Of the 100 mosques surveyed, 51% had texts on site rated as severely advocating violence; 30% had texts rated as moderately advocating violence; and 19% had no violent texts at all. Mosques that presented as Sharia adherent were more likely to feature violence-positive texts on site than were their non-Sharia-adherent counterparts. In 84.5% of the mosques, the imam recommended studying violence-positive texts. The leadership at Sharia-adherent mosques was more likely to recommend that a worshipper study violence-positive texts than leadership at non-Sharia-adherent mosques. Fifty-eight percent of the mosques invited guest imams known to promote violent jihad. The leadership of mosques that featured violence-positive literature was more likely to invite guest imams who were known to promote violent jihad than was the leadership of mosques that did not feature violence-positive literature on mosque premises.

Preface[1]

The debate over the connection between Islam and its legal doctrine and system known as *Sharia* on the one hand and terrorism committed in the name of Islam on the other rages on among counter terrorism professionals, academics, policy experts, theologians, and politicians. Much of this debate centers on the evidence that the perpetrators of violence in the name of Islam source the moral, theological, and legal motivations and justifications for their actions in *Sharia*. Much of the opposition to this focus on *Sharia* centers on the argument that *Sharia* is and has been historically malleable and exploited for good and bad causes.

This study seeks to enter this fray but at a more empirical level. Since we know that mosques are in fact a situs of recruitment and "radicalization" for terrorism committed in the name of Islam, this study seeks to enter into that domain to determine if there is an empirical correlation between actual, manifest *Sharia*-related behaviors and the presence of violent and *jihad*-based literature, and further, the promotion of that literature. While the presence of violent and *jihad*-based literature alone does not necessarily suggest the worshippers at such a mosque adopt the violent literature's approach to the use of violence, if the imams at such mosques also promote the literature, and if those mosques are more likely to invite guest imams and speakers who are known to promote violent *jihad*, the presence of these factors together would be strongly suggestive of an environment prone to *jihad* recruitment. Thus, this study also seeks to determine if the spiritual leadership in these mosques is supportive of this genre of literature.

Introduction

While scholarly inquiry into the root causes and factors supportive of the political violence known as terrorism has accelerated since the September 11, 2001, attacks on the United States; a survey of research in the field reveals a lag in empirical studies that attempt to measure the relationship between specific variables and terrorism phenomena or support for terrorism. Most studies in the field of terrorism research are either based upon anecdotal or retrospective analysis of known data from prior reports of terrorism using multiple regression analysis. [2] Most of these studies disconfirm simplistic causative theories for terrorism, such as socio-economic deprivation. [3]

A 2007 study by Paul Gill noted that prior scholarship had not explored the complex interactions between the individual who becomes a suicide bomber, the terrorist organization that sponsors suicide bombers, and the society that supports the terrorist and terrorist organization. Instead, scholarship had taken a non-integrated approach and previous studies had focused on only one of these three dimensions. [4] The Gill study found, among other things, that the terrorist organization seeks societal support by creating a "culture of martyrdom" and that a theme common to suicide bombers, despite many differences, was that they received support of a community that esteemed the concept of martyrdom. [5] The Gill study advanced scholarship in the area of terrorism research by studying the complex dynamics at work between a terrorist organization, society, and individuals and also proposing that the interplay between those three dimensions enables radicalization and terrorist attacks. [6]

Recent studies, when viewed together, raise the prospect that all three dimensions may be present in highly *Sharia*-adherent mosques, such as those frequented by *Salafists*. This is significant because the mosque would be a convenient locus for making observations and gathering data in an attempt to measure the relationship between specific variables and support for terrorism if all three dimensions that enable radicalization and terrorist attacks are present in these highly *Sharia*-adherent mosques.

A study by Sageman found a connection between highly *Sharia*-adherent *Salafist* Islam and violent *jihad*. This study's authors emphasize that the connection Sageman noticed between Islam and violent *jihad* concerns a particular stream of highly *Sharia*-adherent Islam and not Islam generically. The Sageman study found that 97% of the *jihadists* studied became increasingly devoted to highly *Sharia*-adherent *Salafist* Islam on their path to radicalization despite adhering to various devotional levels during their youths. [7] This noted increase in religious devotion to *Sharia*-adherent *Salafist* Islam was measured by outwardly observable behaviors that are objectively linked to *Sharia*-adherence such as wearing traditional Arabic, Pakistani, or Afghan clothing and growing beards. [8]

The mosque is a societal apparatus that might serve as a support mechanism for the violent *jihad*. Consistent with the findings of the Sageman study, a study conducted by the New York Police Department noted that, in the mosque context, high levels of *Sharia* adherence may relate to support for violent *jihad*. [9] Specifically the NYPD study found that highly *Sharia*-adherent mosques have played a prominent role in radicalizing several groups who conspired to commit acts of terrorism in the name of Islam, including some groups who were successful in carrying out high-profile attacks. [10] One plausible explanation for why the highly *Sharia*-adherent mosque is believed to have a connection to the radicalization process is that the global *jihad* is an

Islamic revivalist movement centered on a common *Sharia*-driven mission[11] and the mosque serves as a locus for the intensification of religious beliefs. [12]

Further raising the profile of highly *Sharia*-adherent mosques is the fact that several of these mosques are known to contain brokers to the violent *jihad*; and in some instances, the broker may even be the mosque's imam. [13] The broker role may also be filled by ostensibly non-violent groups such as the *Tablighi Jamaat*, which counts several alumnae as members of the violent *jihad*. [14] Additionally, these mosques have been the *situs* where other radicals have met "spiritual sanctioners" who foster an "us-versus-them" perspective and provide moral justification for engaging in violent *jihad*. [15] The "spiritual sanctioner" presents *jihad* as a religious duty situated within traditional *Sharia* and the sanctioner's commitment to *jihad* is often the primary determinant of whether a radicalized group will engage in violent *jihad*. [16]

The presence of an imam or other respected member who serves as a "spiritual sanctioner" or even as a broker[17] to *jihad* is critical because a respected Islamic scholar who provides justification for violence against "the other" and presents *jihad* as a religious duty significantly influences the decisions made by one who is seeking a more religiously devout lifestyle. [18] The presence of pro-*jihad* imams and mosque members, and even ostensibly non-violent *Sharia*-advocating groups, serve to support a "culture of martyrdom" by providing moral justification for engaging in violent *jihad* and making available an avenue to participate in violent *jihad*. The presence of groups like the *Tablighi Jamaat*, as well as the presence of individual brokers and "spiritual sanctioners" within the highly *Sharia*-adherent mosques, raises concerns that activities and the atmosphere inside highly *Sharia*-adherent mosques contribute to the creation or maintenance of a "culture of martyrom" where violence and *jihad* are accepted or encouraged.

In addition to the roles played by increased devotion to a highly *Sharia*-adherent strain of Islam, studies have also noticed a connection between violence-positive Islamic literature and violent *jihad*. A study by Quintan Wiktorowicz noted that the modern violent *jihad*, the current avatar of which is Al Qaeda and various groups inspired by Al Qaeda, relies on textual works to legitimize their violent activities. The texts that these *jihadist* groups rely on date from the medieval period, for example works by Ibn Kathir and Ibn Taymiyya, to the modern period, which includes the works of Abul A'la Maududi and Sayyid Qutb. [19] According to Wiktorowicz, violent *Salafists* such as Al Qaeda legitimize their violent activities by applying principles set forth in these texts in ways that take a more expansive and permissive view regarding the use of violence than has been allowed by alternative historical interpretations of these texts. [20] However, Wiktorowicz concedes that under certain circumstances these same texts can be used persuasively to garner the support of otherwise non-violent *Salafists* for the intentional targeting of the American civilian population. [21] Thus, violence-positive texts by Islamic thinkers and exegetes can be exploited not only to sanction engaging in violent *jihad*, but can also be utilized to gain the support of non-violent *Salafists* for the intentional killing of civilians.

These anecdotal studies, when viewed together, suggest that a relationship might be present between high levels of *Sharia* adherence, violence-positive Islamic literature, and institutional support for violence and violent *jihad* within the context of the highly *Sharia*-adherent mosque. The role authoritative, *Sharia*-centric Islam plays in creating or maintaining a culture that manifests behaviors that demonstrate esteem for political violence against an outgroup deserves investigation because the various Islamic terrorist groups and individual *jihadists*, for all their geographic, political, and ideological differences, embrace *Sharia* as their doctrinal legal and political authority for the establishment of a political order or state based on Islamic law as their goal.[22]

Moreover, these Islamic terrorist groups and individual *jihadists* cite *Sharia* as their legal and political justification for the political violence they term *jihad* and those who oppose them term terrorism. To date, almost all of the professional and academic work in the area of terrorism carried out in the name of Islam has been anecdotal surveys or case studies tracing backwards the personal history profiles of different Islamic terrorists and the socio-economic, and political environments from whence they came after the fact (either post mortem or post-capture).[23] There are almost no empirical studies attempting to identify specific behavioral variables (such as various indicia of *Sharia*-adherence) which might positively correlate with behaviors associated with a willingness to tolerate, accept, or even engage in terrorism.

One notable exception to this trend was a group of four studies conducted by Ginges, Hansen, and Norenzayan which sought to measure the association between *religious belief* versus *coalitional commitment* with attitudes directly supportive of terrorism or attitudes suggesting support for terrorism.[24] *Religious belief* was defined and measured by the subject self-reporting his or her frequency of prayer. [25] *Coalitional commitment* was defined and measured by the frequency with which the subject attended communal religious services at a house of worship. [26] The study concluded that a relationship exists between frequency of mosque attendance (coalitional commitment) and the likelihood that a person will support suicide attacks. [27] The study also concluded that there was no empirical evidence to support the religious-belief hypothesis which posits that support for suicide bombings is linked to some measurable index of religious devotion (prayer in this study). [28]

However, the study's methodology as it relates to gathering prayer frequency data may have been susceptible to weakness that introduced bias and led to a faulty conclusion. The study invited over reporting by relying on Muslims to self report their prayer frequency. A Muslim would be under social and/or psychological pressures to over report his prayer frequency because status as a good or pious Muslim is linked to whether a Muslim fulfills his religious obligation to pray five times daily. [29] Status as a good or pious Muslim is not dependent on attending mosque with a high degree of frequency. A Muslim is permitted to pray outside of a mosque environment when necessary. [30] Hence, the pressure to over report, which exists for self-reporting prayer frequency, is not present when a Muslim reports how frequently he or she attends mosque. Moreover, the measure of mosque attendance frequency is both a measure of coalitional commitment and religious devotion.

In the two Palestinian surveys from the Ginges study, 69.3% of the respondents in the first survey and 85% of the respondents in the second survey reported praying five times per day. [31] The results for mosque attendance were more evenly distributed. [32] Thus, the extremely high percentage of respondents who reported praying five times a day makes it difficult to statistically discern whether a correlation exists between the independent variable (prayer frequency) and the dependent variable (support for suicide bombings). While the Ginges study authors disconfirmed the religious-belief hypothesis, a correlation may be shown to exist between indicia of religious devotion and behaviors that increase the likelihood that one is sympathetic to violence once the bias introduced by the self reporting of acts associated with piousness is removed. Indeed, the confirmed hypothesis for coalitional commitment, insofar as mosque attendance is also a measure of religious devotion, suggests the Ginges study authors might have too hastily rejected the religious-belief hypothesis.

A primary purpose of this survey is to pursue the religious-belief hypothesis in the context of praxis, or the measurable adherence to *Sharia*'s legal dictates of prayer worship and dress by Muslim worshippers who are sufficiently devout to pray in mosques. Specifically, this survey seeks to measure whether a correlation exists between measures of religious devotion as defined by certain behaviors objectively linked to *Sharia* adherence, on the one hand, and the presence of violence-positive materials at the mosque, on the other. This study also seeks to measure whether a correlation exists between the presence of violence-positive materials at a mosque and whether the mosque or mosque leadership will promote violence by recommending the study of violence-positive materials, promoting violent *jihad*, or inviting guest speakers who are known to have promoted violent *jihad*. However, this survey avoids the bias that might be introduced through self-reporting resulting from pressure on the respondent to demonstrate his or her piety.

Sharia and the Jurisprudential Consensus Across the Islamic Religio-Legal Schools

Sharia Defined and Its Role in Orthodox Islamic Jurisprudence Explained

Sharia is the Islamic system of law based primarily on two sources held by Muslims to be, respectively, direct revelation from Allah and divinely inspired: the *Quran* and the *Sunnah* (examples and traditions of Muhammad). [33] Additionally, two other sources, *ijma* (scholarly consensus among the accepted *Sharia* authorities -- *ulema*) and *qiyas* (analogy), may be utilized to provide authoritative guidance when the legal rule or solution is not self-evident from the literal text of the *Quran* or *Sunnah*. [34] While *Sharia* law and rulings based on *Sharia* are derived from the same source bodies, *Sharia* is not a monolithic institution. The *Umma*—or Muslim community—is arrayed along several legal, cultural, and nationalistic axes but the deepest legal fault line is the Sunni-Shia divide. Moreover, there are several distinct schools of religio-legal thought contained within both the Sunni and Shia sects. The Sunni sect has given rise to four primary schools of religio-legal thought known as *mathhabs* (or Arabic pl.: *mathahib*): *Hanafi, Shafii, Maliki*, and *Hanbali*. [35] all of which are considered by their respective adherents to be authoritative for their own followers[36] and indeed all permit a fair amount of freedom for adherents to migrate between and among rulings from the different schools. [37] The *Salafi* sects, such as the *Wahhabi* groups based mostly in the Arabian Peninsula, and the *Deobandis* based mostly in Pakistan and India, are also considered a distinct and legitimate approach to *Sharia* by most Sunni legal scholars.[38] Within Shia Islam, there are three primary *mathhabs*: *Ithna-Ashari, Zayadi*, and *Ismaili*.[39]

The differences among the legal schools are typically understood to exist at one of two levels. The first is at the level of positive law, or the definitive rulings on any given question typically answered in a scholar's ruling called a *fatwa*. This is typically referred to as the *fiqh*. The second distinction among the legal schools is found in the very jurisprudential methodology purportedly operating as the source for discovering the law. This is typically referred to as *usul al fiqh*, or the science of the law.[40]

In the first instance, diversity of the normative legal rulings of the *fiqh* across the *mathhabs* is illustrated in matters of personal status, for example the varying approaches in the areas of divorce and temporary marriage. Concerning divorce, *Hanafi* interpretation allows a woman to apply for a divorce when her husband is unable to consummate the marriage, but the other Sunni *mathhabs* require that a wife pay a sum before being released from marriage. [41] With regard to the concept of "temporary marriage," the Shia *Ithna-Ashari* school allows for "temporary marriage" while none of its Sunni counterparts recognize the practice. [42]

While there is room for these differences in the normative rulings of the *fiqh* between the various *mathhabs* in the Sunni world, and between the Sunni and Shia legal rulings, the divergence at the level of positive law is, given the fullness of the *corpus juris* of the *fiqh*, confined to relatively few issues and to ones that operate generally at the margins. Thus, there is unity and agreement across the Sunni-Shia split and across the various Sunni *mathhabs* on the core *Sharia* normative precepts that form the essentials of orthodox Islamic jurisprudence. The introduction to *Reliance of the Traveller* makes prominent note of the fact that the Sunni *mathhabs* are "identical in approximately 75 percent of their legal conclusions" and that differences among the four Sunni *mathhabs* are attributable to differences in methodology—not ideology. [43] This consistency and agreement on core *Sharia* rulings not only extend across the Sunni *matthabs*, but also bridge the Sunni-Shia divide. Thus, in a 1959 fatwa, the head of the preeminent Sunni university, Al-Azhar in Cairo, Egypt, ruled that the Shia *Ithna-Ashari* mathhab was as religiously valid to follow as any of the recognized Sunni *matthabs*; and going further, the fatwa stated that transferring from one recognized *matthab* to another was no crime. [44] More recently, *The Amman Message* echoed the view that all major *matthabs* are legitimate, that the followers of these major *matthabs* may not be declared apostate, and that the major schools of Islamic thought express agreement on fundamental Islamic principles. [45] Presumably, if the normative rulings across the Sunni-Shia divide were inapposite on a majority of issues or on core issues, the leading Sunni legal authorities would not have granted Shia *fiqh* this prestigious standing, especially in light of the theological differences which have divided the Sunni and Shia sects historically.

The reason for this generous uniformity within the *corpus* of positive law rulings among the *ulema* of the various legal schools is a question for legal historians and possibly forensic anthropologists. The fact of this broad consensus, however, is indisputable. Interestingly, though, the differences in *usul al fiqh*, or the jurisprudential methodology said to underlie the normative rulings of the *fiqh*, are much greater. While this is true across the Sunni legal schools, it is unmistakably the case across the Sunni-Shia divide. While there are considerable similarities in the *usul al fiqh* of the Sunni and Shia worlds, it is fair to say that the standing of the Imamate in Shia methodology creates a difference operating at the core of methodology. [46]

This leads to an anomaly of sorts. If the methodologies between the Sunni-Shia axis are so starkly distinguishable, how is it that the normative rulings of the *fiqh* remain remarkably aligned? One scholar who has examined this anomaly has suggested that historically the articulated methodologies of the various legal schools represented by *usul al fiqh* in fact followed the actual development of the *fiqh*—representing a kind of *ex post facto* rationalization. Indeed, he suggests that even after the emergence of clearly articulated methodologies of the various legal schools, with clear divergences amongst them, the normative rulings of the *fiqh* continued within the pre-existent consensus. [47]

Violent Jihad is an Integral Part of Orthodox Sharia-Centric Islam

The propriety of violent *jihad*, expressed as kinetic warfare against non-Muslims, is a matter that finds agreement in orthodox Islamic, *Sharia* materials and Islamic tradition. This is true even though there is no universally accepted single doctrine of *jihad*. [48] *Jihad and the Islamic Law of War* notes that there are adherents to Islam of both Sunni and Shia extraction who believe that all non-Muslims, as well as those Muslims who are insufficiently devout, are legitimate targets for violence. [49] *Takfiri* and *jihadist* are the terms used to describe this group of militant Islamic fundamentalists. *[50]*

Jihad can be divided into two basic categories—defensive *jihad* and offensive *jihad*—each with its own implications for the Islamic community and individual Muslims. [51] Offensive *jihad* is waged to expand the territory controlled by Islam and is declared by the Caliph. [52] Defensive *jihad* is waged when lands under Islamic control are attacked by non-Muslim forces. [53] Defensive *jihad* is an individual obligation (*fard 'ayn*) incumbent on, at a minimum, every Muslim in the Muslim land under attack, and at a maximum, every Muslim globally to support the *jihad* by fighting, praying, or making financial contributions to the *jihad*. [54] In the modern era, with the conspicuous absence of a recognized Caliph, the issue of offensive *jihad* remains a doctrine with nebulous practical implications. Modern *jihads* are almost always characterized as defensive *jihads*, but it is also the case that the line between a defensive *jihad* and an offensive one is blurry at best given a world in which Muslim countries invariably interact with and often submit to the will of non-Muslim denominated countries and powers as a matter of international law and relations and judicial and diplomatic comity. [55]

The authors of *Jihad and the Islamic Law of War* speak derisively of the *Takfirist* approach taken by Osama bin Laden, the avatar of the modern *jihad* movement, accusing him and those like him of ignoring traditional Islamic law and relying selectively on only sources that support the conclusions desired by bin Laden and similar actors. [56] These authors argue that traditional Islamic law and its precedents act as a restraint against the illegal use of force and that traditional Islamic law does not permit non-combatants to be viewed as legitimate targets. [57]

A careful reading, however, of classical, orthodox Islamic exegetical and legal materials reveals that modern *jihadists* or *takfiris* have at least a colorable claim under orthodox *Sharia* sources, and historical precedent, to conduct the *jihad* they wage; and this includes the intentional targeting and killing of non-combatants. The classic and still highly authoritative *Sharia* exegetical resource, *Tafsir Ibn Kathir*, exhorts Muslims on several occasions to wage *jihad* and places few, if any, restrictions on how and when to conduct *jihad*. [58] The classical works of several respected jurists and scholars from the four Sunni *mathhabs* dating from the 8th to 14th centuries are all in agreement that violent *jihad* against non-Muslims is an obligation incumbent on Muslims. [59] Moreover, the respected classical jurist, Al-Shaybani, who was a disciple of the founder of the Sunni *Hanafi matthab*, advised that it was lawful for a group of Muslims to attack non-Muslims in areas controlled by non-Muslims even without the approval of the Islamic *Caliph.* [60] Further, Shaybani advised that it was acceptable to kill non-Muslim prisoners of war and non-combatant civilians. [61]

Indeed, this pedigree for a rather full-throated *jihad* against the non-Muslim world has been noted by an important scholar in one of the first published works post-9/11 attempting to actually parse the modern doctrine of *jihad* by noting its roots in classical *fiqh.* Thus, Mary Habeck's *Knowing the Enemy* correctly notes:

The question of offensive jihad is even more complex and controversial. The most widely respected Islamic authorities: the six accepted collections of (Sunni) hadith; the authoritative commentators on, and exegetes of, the hadith and Qur'an; the leading ancient experts on Islamic law; and the four schools of Islamic fiqh all assume that Muslims have a duty to spread the dominion of Islam, through military offensives, until it rules the world. [62]

Directing violence against others on the basis of their status as non-Muslims as a normative, legally-sanctioned behavior is not a concept confined to Islam's distant history, but is also an accepted feature of modern orthodox, *Sharia*-centric Islam. Al-Azhar University, in its 1991 certification of an English translation of the classical manual, *Reliance of the Traveller,* stated that the English translation "conforms to the practice and faith of the orthodox Sunni community." [63] The translation certified by Al-Azhar University as conforming to orthodox Sunni practice, spends eleven pages discussing *jihad* as violence directed against non-Muslims. [64] Providing modern Shiite support for the concept of *jihad* as violence against non-Muslims, the prominent Shia authority and ruler Ayatollah Ruhollah Khomeini is recorded as saying,

Islam says: Kill them [the non-Muslims], put them to the sword and scatter [their armies]. ... People cannot be made obedient except with the sword! The sword is the key to Paradise, which can be opened only for the Holy Warriors! There are hundreds of other [Qur'anic] psalms and Hadiths [sayings of the Prophet] urging Muslims to value war and to fight. Does all this mean that Islam is a religion that prevents men from waging war? I spit upon those foolish souls who make such a claim. [65]

Therefore, while *Sharia* has room for a difference of opinion on some matters, the Islamic religio-legal schools express unity for core Islamic principles, which operates in a *de jure* and *de facto* manner as authoritative *ijma* or consensus. Additionally, as discussed above, violent *jihad* employed on the basis of the target's religious identity or practice is a concept that receives support from both Sunni and Shia legal authorities and this support is not confined to medieval literature, but is an idea that has also been advanced by prominent modern Islamic legal scholars and ideological leaders.

Methodology & Data Analysis

Sampling

The survey analyzed data collected from a random sample of 100 mosques. This sample size provided sufficient statistical power to find a modest significant association between the *Sharia* adherence and violence-positive variables. A sample size of 100 mosques also allowed the survey to extrapolate to all mosques in the United States at a 95% confidence interval with a margin of error of +/-9.6%. State-by-state estimates of the Muslim population were extracted from the only extant such survey[66] and used to create a listing of all states whose Muslim population represented at least 1% of the estimated total United States Muslim population. The final listing was comprised of eighteen states and the District of Columbia. [67] Fourteen states and the District of Columbia ("15 randomly selected states") were randomly selected from the final listing to accommodate limits on physical logistics and personnel resources. The study built a comprehensive list of mosques that could be located and surveyed in these 15 randomly selected states. The process is described in greater detail below.

The survey developed a site list of mosques located in each of the 15 randomly selected states after consulting several resources in order to build the most comprehensive list of existing mosques as possible. First, the survey combined the data on the 1,209 mosques listed in "Mosque in America: A National Portrait" [68] with the data on the 1,659 mosques obtained online from Harvard's Pluralism Project. [69] After the mosque lists from the two sources were combined, a review was conducted to ensure that each mosque address was not listed twice. If it was found, during the review, that a mosque address was listed twice, then one of the two addresses was removed from the mosque listing prior to the random selection process. The survey then identified the cities in each state where the highest concentrations of Muslims lived based on open source information relating Muslim demographics for each of the 15 randomly selected states. Additional mosques were located and added to the list by consulting telephone books, gathering information at existing mosques, and conducting visual field inspections. A Friday telephone call was made to every mosque on the site list in order to confirm the mosque's existence prior to sending a researcher for an onsite visit. Friday was selected as the day to attempt telephone contact because an employee or representative would most likely be present at mosque on that day. A mosque was excluded from the list if either it did not have a valid telephone number or its telephone remained unanswered after three Friday telephone calls. The final mosque site list for the 15 randomly selected states yielded a total of 1,401 mosques. The first 100 mosques on the site list were selected and arranged by metropolitan area. All remaining mosques were grouped by metropolitan area and then randomized.

The dates and prayer times (noon [*Dhuhr*]; afternoon [*'Asr*]; sunset [*Maghrib*]; and evening [*'Isha*]) for any given mosque surveyed were randomly selected. The randomly selected dates and times included both weekday and Friday prayers (the *Jumu'ah*). If the surveyor went to a mosque for a prayer service but found the mosque closed, abandoned, or was unable to locate the mosque at the address provided on the mosque site list, the next mosque that appeared on the randomized list for that city was chosen one after the other until the surveyor located a mosque that was open for the prayer service.

Prepatory Data Collection

The initial mosque visits were conducted between May 18, 2007, and December 4, 2008 ("Survey Period") by surveyors who visited mosques. Each of the mosques visited during the Survey Period were visited again between May 10, 2009, and May 30, 2010 ("Audit Period") to audit the findings of the Survey Period. The results of the Audit Period confirmed the findings in the Survey Period in all but nine mosques. Of these nine, four had closed or moved to an unknown location; the remaining five mosques had additional or different texts available. Of the four closed mosques, the next available mosque for that city on the random list was chosen for the survey. Of the five mosques which presented different texts during the Audit Period, surveyors visited the mosque on a third visit and recorded the findings. Only those texts available on two of the three visits were recorded as present.

Prior to visiting a mosque, a surveyor would obtain as much open source information about the mosque as possible. There were two primary open sources used to obtain mosque information: the Internet and materials from or about the subject mosque that were gathered when surveyors previously visited other mosques. When the dominant language of the subject mosque was determined to be other than English, such as Arabic, Urdu, or Farsi, the surveyor who visited the mosque was fluent in that language.

Survey Procedure

Mosque visits were conducted during the Survey Period and the Audit Period. Each mosque visit included attending and observing a prayer service and surveying materials distributed and texts made available on mosque premises. Additionally, the imam (or senior lay leader if no imam was present) was asked what materials he would recommend for further study. The surveyors recorded their observations on an instrument designed for the survey.

Instrument[70]

The surveyor completed the survey instrument which included noting the location, date, time of visit, type of structure (stand alone, store front, etc.), estimated number of worshipers, whether any of the following texts were present and represented at least 10% of the texts made available: books authored by Abul A'la Maududi or Sayyid Qutb; *Sharia* legal texts *Fiqh-us-Sunnah* or *Riyad-us-Saliheen*, and the *Quranic* commentary of *Tafsir Ibn Kathir*. The surveyor also noted the presence of other materials including texts, pamphlets, handouts, audio and video recordings, titles, and authors (if available). When the materials were provided to the surveyor to retain, the materials were collected and retained for further research. When not, the surveyor noted the substance of the material to the extent possible.

A section of 13 items on strictness of *Sharia* adherence was completed, which included: segregation of the sexes, prayer line alignment, garb and beard of imam and of worshipers, all of which are objectively linked to *Sharia* adherence. In addition, a section of 22 items rated materials pertaining to violent *jihad*, which included the promotion of violent *jihad* or the encouragement to join a *jihad* organization, the collection of funds supporting *jihad*, the promotion of violence in the service of *Sharia*, the distribution of memorabilia glorifying violent *jihad*, the presence of materials indicating that imams known to promote violent *jihad* were invited to speak as guest imams at the mosque, and whether violent *jihad* materials were distributed for free. Where possible, the surveyor recorded whether the imam recommended such materials. If the imam either recommended or unenthusiastically recommended the study of any violence-positive materials to one who presented as a new worshipper, then the surveyor recorded the imam as having recommended violence-positive materials. If the imam either did not recommend the study of and violence-positive materials to one who presented as a new worshipper or instructed against the study of violence-positive materials, then the surveyor recorded that the imam did not recommend the study of violence-positive materials.

Variable Selection

Behavior Variables [71]

Behavior variables were selected according to those behaviors that doctrinal, traditional *Sharia* adherents contend were exhibited and commanded by Muhammad as recorded in the *Sunna*; and, later discussed and preserved in *Sharia* literature such as *Reliance of the Traveller* and *Fiqh-us-Sunnah*. The behaviors selected enjoy sanction by authoritative Islamic sources such as *Reliance of the Traveller*—which as previously noted conforms to the practice of orthodox Sunni Islam—and as such, the selected behaviors are among the most broadly accepted by legal practitioners of Islam and are not those behaviors practiced only by a rigid sub-group within Islam—*Salafists* for example.

The selected behaviors were observable in the mosque environment; and, therefore, empirically measurable. The behaviors noted as being *Sharia* adherent are outward manifestations of internalized beliefs or commitments as praxes. These *Sharia*-adherent behaviors were selected precisely because they constitute observable and measurable praxes of an orthodox form of Islam; and were not merely internalized, non-observable articles of faith.

Among the mosque behaviors observed and scored as *Sharia* adherent were: (a) women wearing the *hijab*; (b) gender segregation during mosque prayers; and (c) enforcement of prayer lines. As previously mentioned, the behaviors were selected to be scored as *Sharia* adherent because they both enjoy sanction in authoritative *Sharia* literature and are practices that enjoy broad acceptance within Islamic orthodoxy. For example, *Reliance of the Traveller* and *Fiqh-us-Sunnah* express agreement on the obligation of a woman to wear the *hijab*. Excerpts from both authorities outlining the woman's obligation to wear the *hijab* follow:

There is no such dispute over what constitutes a woman's '*aurah* [private parts/nakedness]. It is stated that her entire body is '*aurah* and must be covered, except her hands and face. ... Allah does not accept the prayer of an adult woman unless she is wearing a headcovering (*khimar*, *hijab*).[72]

The nakedness of a woman (O: even if a young girl) consists of the whole body except the face and hands. (N. The nakedness of woman is that which invalidates the prayer if exposed (dis:w23). [73] ... It is recommended for a woman to wear a covering over her head (*khimar*), a full length shift, and a heavy slip under it that does not cling to the body. [74]

The *Sharia* literature also expresses similar agreement on the requirement that the genders be separated during prayers. For example, both *Reliance of the Traveller* and *Fiqh-us-Sunnah* express a preference that women should pray at home rather than at the mosque. [75] However, both sources further agree that if women do pray in the mosque, then they should pray in lines separate from the men's prayer lines.[76] Additionally, authoritative *Sharia* literature agrees that the men's prayer lines should be straight, that the men should be close together in their prayer lines, and that the imam should enforce alignment of the men's prayer lines. [77]

The fact that not all Muslims adhere to a completely *Sharia*-adherent lifestyle and not all mosques conduct their religious services in conformity with normative *Sharia* dictates allowed surveyors to observe and record variations in *Sharia* adherence levels among the mosques surveyed and the individuals who attended these mosques This study borrowed from the analytical framework suggested by *Jihad and the Islamic Law of War*, which describes and categorizes—from extreme secularism to extreme sectarianism—the adherence levels of the world's Muslims.[78] Muslims who embrace secularism and modernism are referred to as "secular fundamentalists" and "modern secularists."[79] Muslims who fit into these categories— at a minimum—view Western values and civilization as "the 'norm' to which the Islamic world should adjust itself." [80] The extreme sectarian end of the Islamic adherence spectrum are occupied by Muslims who fit into the categories of "Puritanical literalist," also referred to as *Salafist*, and sometimes in the less precise political terms "Islamist" and *"Takfiri"* or *jihadist*.[81] Muslims who would be categorized as Puritanical literalists seek to duplicate the state created by Muhammad and rid society of elements that are not consistent with the earliest Muslim community.[82] A *Takfiri* is a Muslim who views non-Muslims and those who—in his opinion— are insufficiently devout as unbelievers and legitimate targets for violence.[83] Resting in between these two extremes are the Muslims categorized as "Traditionalists" who look to *Sharia* as a legal and normative structure to inform them how to conduct their affairs—both their inward and outward lives, but who might not adhere to all of its dictates literally. [84]

Surveyors observed the conduct of mosque services and the behavioral choices of worshippers at a given mosque, and then scored the observed behaviors as *Sharia* adherent if the behaviors were objectively linked to normative *Sharia* behaviors, as recorded in the *Quran* or *Haddith* and confirmed as such by extant and authoritative *Sharia* literature, or were behaviors that are understood as being preferred behaviors among a consensus of *Sharia* scholars. Given that *Jihad and the Islamic Law of War* divided the Muslim world into two basic camps—(a) those who believe the West should conform to traditional Islamic or *Sharia* norms and who embrace and practice *Sharia* in their personal lives and (b) those who largely or entirely reject traditional Islamic or *Sharia* norms and do not practice *Sharia* in their personal lives—the surveyors scored the observed behaviors and conduct of mosque services as being either *Sharia* adherent or not *Sharia* adherent. The mosques where the highest degrees of *Sharia* adherence were observed were the *Salafi-Wahabi* and *Deobandi* mosques. The levels of *Sharia* adherence decreased until there were minimally observed or no indicia of what could be thought of as "traditional" or "orthodox" *Sharia* adherence.

Texts Selected

Texts were selected for scoring based on the fact that they either called for violent *jihad* against non-Muslims or because the texts called for hatred of "the other." For example, *Reliance of the Traveller* is a selected text because it makes explicit demands for *jihad* against non-Muslims. A sampling of quotes on *jihad* and the non-Muslim from *Reliance of the Traveller*:

The caliph (o25) makes war upon Jews, Christians, and Zoroastrians (N: provided he has first invited them to enter Islam in faith and practice, and if they will not, then invited them to enter the social order of Islam by paying the non-Muslim poll tax (*jizya*, def: o11.4)... [85]

The caliph fights all other peoples until they become Muslim (O: because they are not a people with a Book, nor honored as such, and are not permitted to settle with paying the poll tax (*jizya*)). [86]

The *Fiqh-us-Sunnah* and *Tafsir Ibn Kathir* were among the other books which were selected for scoring based on their promotion of violence against and hatred of "the other." A sample quote from both *Fiqh-us-Sunnah* and *Tafsir Ibn Kathir* follows:

Ibn 'Abbas reported that the Prophet, upon whom be peace, said, 'The ties of Islam and the principles of the religion are three, and whoever leaves one of them becomes an unbeliever, and his blood becomes lawful: testifying that there is no god except Allah, the obligatory prayers, and the fast of Ramadan.' (Related by Abu Ya'la with a hassan chain.) Another narration states, 'If anyone leaves one of [the three principles], by Allah he becomes an unbeliever and no voluntary deeds or recompense will be accepted from him, and his blood and wealth become lawful.' This is a clear indication that such a person is to be killed. [87]

Perform *jihad* against the disbelievers with the sword and be harsh with the hypocrites with words, and this is the *jihad* performed against them. [88]

Texts authored by Maududi and Qutb and similar materials, such as pamphlets and texts published and disseminated by the Muslim Brotherhood, were selected in part because these materials strongly advocate the use of violence as a means to establish an Islamic state. Maududi espoused that it was legitimate to direct violent *jihad* against "infidel colonizers" in order to gain independence and spread *Sharia*-centric Islam. [89] In the below excerpt from *Jihad in Islam*, Maududi explained the Islamic duty to employ force in pursuit of a *Sharia*-based order:

These [Muslim] men who propagate religion are not mere preachers or missionaries, but the functionaries of God, (so that they may be witnesses for the people), and it is their duty to wipe out oppression, mischief, strife, immorality, high handedness and unlawful exploitation from the world by force of arms. [90]

The ideas in Qutb's *Milestones* serve as the political and ideological backbone of the current global *jihad* movement. [91] In the quote below from *Milestones*, Qutb explains that violence must be employed against those who stand in the way of Islam's expansion:

If someone does this [prevents others from accepting Islam], then it is the duty of Islam to fight him until either he is killed or until he declares his submission. [92]

While works by Maududi and Qutb, as well as similar materials, were selected because of their strong endorsements of violence, these works were also selected because they help to contemporize the view that violent *jihad* is a legitimate vehicle for Islamic expansionism. This is especially true of Qutb whose ideas profoundly influenced the Muslim Brotherhood and Al-Qaeda, the latter through its co-founder, Ayman Al-Zawahiri. [93]

These severe-rated violence-positive materials by Maududi, Qutb, and others distinguish themselves from the moderate-rated violence-positive materials because they are not Islamic legal texts per se, but rather polemical works seeking to advance a politicized Islam through violence, if necessary. Further, the authors of these severe-rated materials were not recognized *Sharia* scholars. Works such as *Tafsir Ibn Kathir*, *Reliance of the Traveller*, and *Fiqh-us-Sunnah* are Islamic legal and exegetical resources written by respected *Sharia* scholars. *Tafsir Ibn*

Kathir, *Reliance of the Traveller*, *Fiqh-us-Sunnah* and similar works contain passages exhorting readers to commit violence against non-Muslims as a means to further an expansionist view of Islam. However, they also contain detailed instructions regarding how a Muslim should order his or her daily routine in order to demonstrate his or her piety to the Muslim community and to Islam's god.

This is especially true of the *Fiqh-us-Sunnah* which focused primarily on the internal Muslim community, family and individual believer, and did not frame *jihad* as an open-ended, divinely ordained imperative. Relatively speaking, the *Fiqh-us-Sunnah* expressed a very restrained view of violent *jihad* in comparison to the other rated materials. The text does not explicitly call for violent *jihad* against the West even though the text understands Western influence of Islamic governments as a force that is destructive to Islam itself. [94] The moderate-rated exegetical and legal materials were written by respected *Sharia* scholars—and although they express positive views toward the use of violence against "the other"—there may be legitimate, non-violent religious purposes to support their presence on mosque premises. By contrast, the severe-rated materials by Maududi, Qutb, and others were not primarily concerned with instructing Muslims on the mundane aspects of daily living, but rather on imparting a global view of Islam through polemical works extolling violent *jihad*.

Data Analysis

The first round of analysis was descriptive to allow presenting a profile of the mosques. The second round of analysis examined the association between *Sharia* adherence and key mosque, imam, and worshiper characteristics. The third round of analysis examined the association of texts recommended by the imam for study and the same key characteristics. To facilitate conducting the above analyses, a three-point scale of strictness of adherence of texts to *Sharia* and advocating the use of violence in the pursuit of a *Sharia*-based political order, including praising the use of violent *jihad* against the West and the use of violence to implement *Sharia*, was created. Based on an empirical analysis of texts (available upon request from authors), from most severe to least severe texts: (1) texts authored by Abul A'la Maududi, Sayyid Qutb, or other similar texts, and the *Sharia* legal text *Riyad-us-Saliheen*; (2) *Quranic* commentary of *Tafsir Ibn Kathir* and the *Sharia* legal text *Fiqh-us-Sunnah*, and (3) having no such texts. The association of the scale and *Sharia* adherence items were then examined using crosstabs with chi-square and a test of linearity for ordinal variables and analysis of variance for continuous variables. Similarly, we examined the association of key characteristics and whether or not the imam or lay leader recommended such materials that advocate the use of violence in the pursuit of a *Sharia*-based political order.

Results[95]

Violence-positive materials were found in a very large majority (81%) of the 100 mosques surveyed. Violence-positive materials were more likely to be found in mosques whose communal prayer practices, imams, and adult male worshipers exhibited greater indicia of *Sharia*-adherent behaviors than were their less *Sharia*-adherent counterparts. Moreover, the mosques that contained violence-positive materials were many times more likely than mosques that did not contain violence-positive materials to engage in several behaviors that promoted violence and violent jihad.

Association of Sharia Observance in Mosque Prayer Observance and Imam Appearance to the Presence of Violence-Positive Materials and Whether the Imam Recommended the Study of Violence-Positive Materials

Mosques that conducted their communal prayers in accordance with *Sharia* advocated norms were more likely to contain violence-positive materials, both moderate and severe, than those mosques whose communal prayer practices did not conform to *Sharia* norms.

Almost all of the mosques that engaged in gender segregation during prayer service, as advocated by *Sharia*, contained violence-positive texts on their premises. Sixty percent (60%) of the mosques that engaged in gender segregation contained severe materials; 35% contained moderate materials; and 5% contained no violence-positive materials. Mosques that did not segregate women from men during communal prayer were more likely than mosques that segregated men from women to contain no materials (26%); and were less likely to contain moderate materials (27%) or severe materials (47%).

In addition to containing violence-positive materials, mosques that engaged in gender segregation during communal prayer services were more likely to be led by imams who recommended that worshipers study violence-positive materials than were mosques that did not engage in gender segregation during communal prayer. Ninety-four percent (94%) of the imams at mosques that engaged in gender segregation recommended that worshipers study violence-positive materials; while only 6% did not recommend that worshipers study violence-positive materials. Imams who led mosques that did not engage in gender segregation were less likely than the imams of mosques that segregated men from women during prayers to recommend that worshipers study violence-positive materials. Eighty percent (80%) of the imams who led congregations that did not engage in gender segregation during prayers recommended that worshipers study violence-positive materials; and 20% of these imams did not recommend that worshipers study such materials.

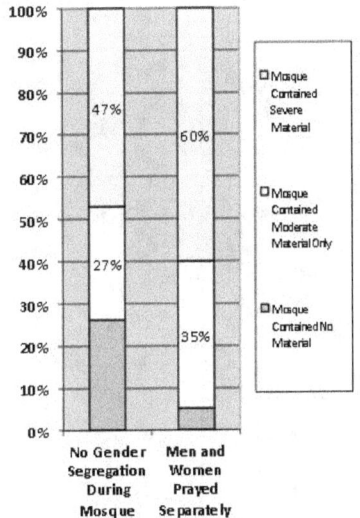

Association of Gender Segregation During Mosque Prayer and the Severity of Materials Found on Mosques' Premises

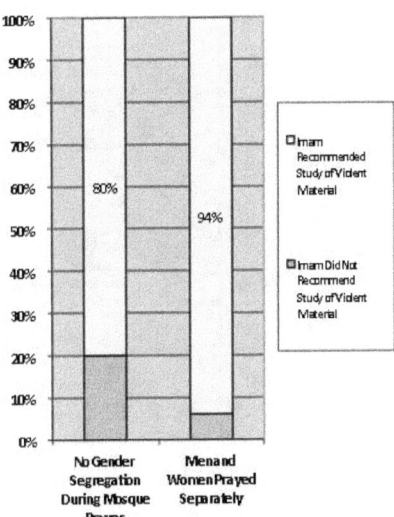

Association of Gender Segregation During Mosque Prayer and Whether the Imams Recommended the Study of Violence-Positive Materials

Mosques that had either a layperson or an imam enforce alignment of the men's prayer lines were more likely to contain violence-positive materials than were mosques that did not enforce the alignment of men's prayer lines. Of the mosques that enforced alignment of men's prayer lines, 59% contained severe materials; 37% contained moderate materials; and 4% contained no violence-positive materials. Forty-two percent (42%) of the mosques that paid little attention to men's prayer line alignment contained severe materials; 22% contained moderate materials; and 36% contained no materials.

Mosques that enforced alignment of men's prayer lines were more likely to be led by an imam who recommended that worshipers study violence positive materials than were mosques that did not enforce men's prayer line alignment. Imams of 96% of the mosques that enforced men's prayer line alignment recommended the study of violence-positive materials and only 4% did not recommend the study of such materials. Imams at 72% of the mosques that did not enforce alignment of men's prayer lines recommended that worshipers study violence-positive materials while 28% of the imams at these mosques did not recommend that worshipers study violence-positive materials.

Association of Alignment of Men's Prayer
Lines and the Severity of Materials Found
on Mosques' Premises

Association of Alignment of Men's Prayer
Lines and Whether the Imams
Recommended the Study of Violence-
Positive Materials

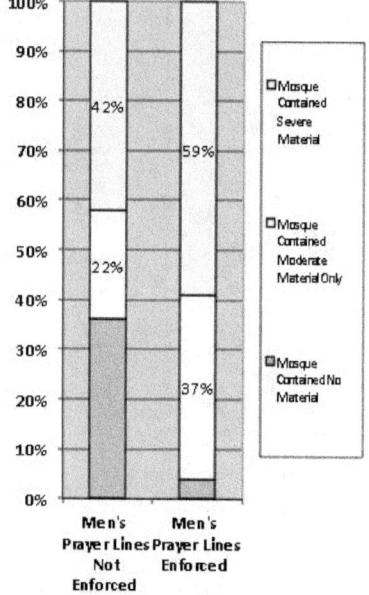
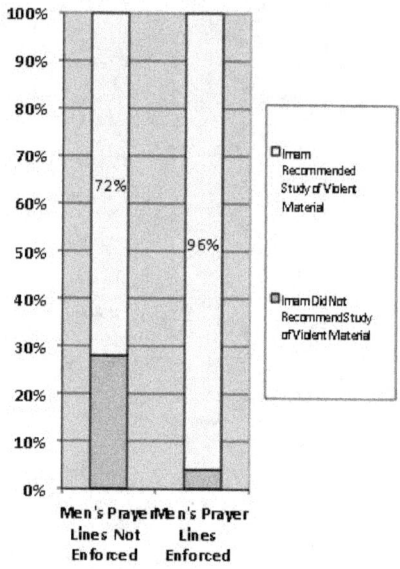

Similar to gender segregation during prayer service and enforcement of men's prayer lines, the imams' choice of beard was also related to the presence of violence-positive materials on mosque property and whether the imam would recommend the study of violence-positive materials. Sixty-one percent (61%) of mosques led by an imam who wore a Sunna beard contained severe materials; 33% contained moderate materials; and 7% contained no violence-positive materials. Mosques led by an imam who did not wear a Sunna beard were less likely to contain severe materials and more likely to contain no violence-positive materials than the mosques led by imams who wore a Sunna beard. Forty-six percent (46%) of mosques led by an imam who did not wear a Sunna beard contained severe materials; 28% contained moderate materials; and 26% contained no violence-positive materials. Imams who wore a Sunna beard were more likely to recommend that worshipers study violence-positive materials than were imams who did not wear a Sunna beard. Of the imams who wore a Sunna beard, 93% recommended that worshipers study violence-positive materials and 7% did not recommend worshipers study violence-positive materials. Seventy-eight percent (78%) of imams who did not wear a Sunna beard recommended that worshipers study violence-positive materials; and 22% did not recommend worshipers study violence-positive materials.

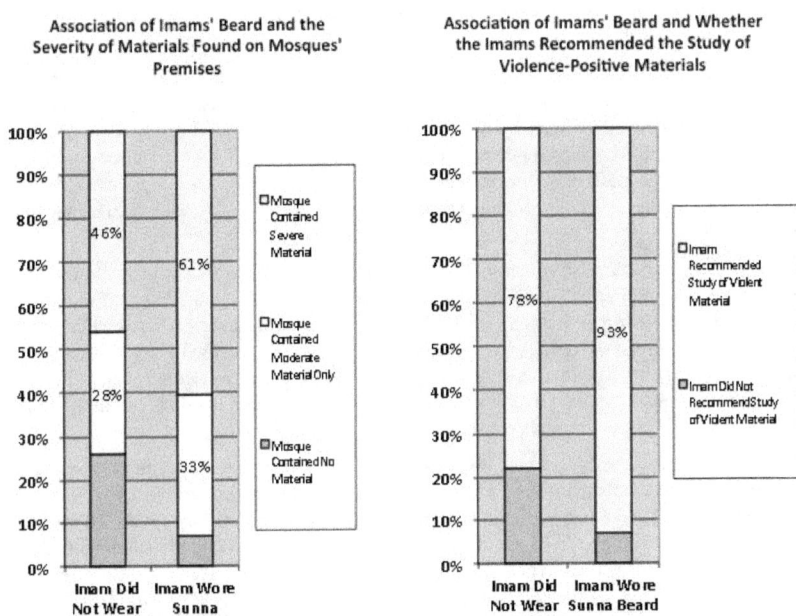

Other measures of the imams' *Sharia* adherence—whether the imam wore a head covering; whether the imam wore traditional, or non-Western garb; and whether an imam wore his watch on his right wrist—were also indicative of whether a mosque would be more likely to contain violence-positive materials than mosques where the imam did not practice these *Sharia*-adherent behaviors. However, the relationship between these behaviors and the presence of violence-positive materials was not statistically significant.

Mosques led by imams who wore a religious head covering were more likely to contain violence-positive materials than mosques that were led by imams who did not wear a religious head covering. Of the mosques led by imams who wore a religious head covering, 60% contained severe materials; 26% contained moderate materials; and 14% contained no violence-positive materials. Of the mosques led by imams who did not wear a religious head covering, 46% contained severe materials; 35% contained moderate materials; and 20% contained no violence-positive materials.

Mosques led by imams who wore traditional Islamic clothing were more likely to contain violence-positive materials than were mosques led by imams who wore Western clothing. Of mosques led by imams who wore traditional Islamic clothing, 62% contained severe materials; 29% contained moderate materials; and 10% contained no violence-positive materials. Of mosques led by imams who wore Western clothing, 43% contained severe materials; 32% contained moderate materials; and 25% no violence-positive materials.

Mosques led by imams who wore a watch on their right wrist were more likely to contain violence-positive materials than mosques led by imams who did not wear a watch on their right wrist. Of the mosques led by imams who wore a watch on their right wrist, 42% contained severe materials; 50% contained moderate materials; and 8% contained no violence-positive materials. Of the mosques led by imams who did not wear a watch on their right wrist, 54% contained severe materials; 28% contained moderate materials; and 18% contained no violence-positive materials.

These same measures of *Sharia* adherence by a mosque's imam were also indicative of whether the imam would recommend that a worshiper study violence-positive materials. Of the three behaviors, the relationship between an imam wearing traditional Islamic garb and whether an imam would recommend the study of violence-positive materials was the only statistically significant relationship. The relationship between both (a) an imam wearing a head covering and (b) an imam wearing a watch on his right hand and whether an imam would recommend the study of violence-positive materials was not statistically significant.

Imams who wore head coverings were more likely to recommend that a worshiper study violence-positive materials than were imams who did not wear head coverings. Ninety percent (90%) of imams who wore head coverings recommended that worshipers study violence-positive materials. Eighty percent (80%) of imams who did not wear head coverings recommended the study of violence-positive materials.

Imams who wore traditional Islamic clothing were more likely to recommend the study of violence-positive materials than were imams who wore Western garb. Of the imams who wore traditional Islamic dress, 92% recommended the study of violence-positive materials. Seventy-seven percent (77%) of the imams who wore Western garb recommended worshipers study violence-positive materials.

Association of Worshipers Sharia-Based Appearance Characteristics to the Presence of Violence-Positive Materials and Whether the Imam Recommended the Study of Violence-Positive Materials

The severity of violence-positive materials present on mosque premises increased as the percentage of adult male worshipers who exhibited *Sharia*-adherent appearance characteristics increased. In mosques where no violence-positive material was found, an average of 14% of the men wore beards. An average of 36% of the men wore beards at mosques where only moderate materials were found; and an average of 48% of the men wore beards at mosques that contained severe materials.

In mosques where no violence-positive materials were found, an average of 16% of the men wore religious hats. An average of 34% of the men wore religious hats at mosques where only moderate materials were found; and an average of 47% of the men wore religious hats at mosques that contained severe materials.

A negative relationship was shown to exist between adult male worshipers exhibiting a Western or assimilative appearance the presence of violence-positive materials on mosque premises. In mosques where no violence-positive materials were found, an average of 73% of the men wore Western garb. An average of 35% of the men wore Western garb at mosques that contained only moderate materials; and an average of 34% of the men wore Western garb at those mosques that contained severe materials.

Association of Adult Male Worshiper Characteristics and the Severity of Violence-Positive Materials Found on Mosques' Premises

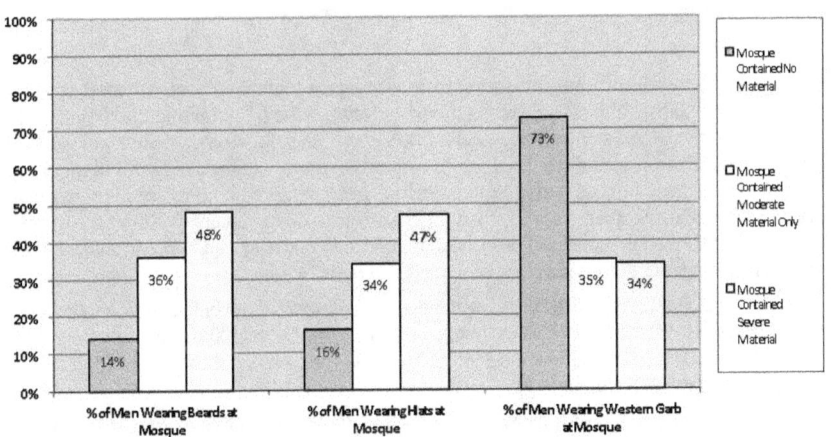

The mosques where imams recommended the study of violence-positive materials were marked by higher percentages of adult male worshipers who exhibited *Sharia*-adherent appearance characteristics and lower percentages of adult males who wore Western, assimilative clothing than those mosques where the imam did not recommend the study of violence-positive materials. In mosques led by an imam who recommended the study of violence-positive materials, 44% of the adult male worshipers wore beards; 42% wore religious hats; and 34% wore Western clothing. In mosques led by an imam who did not recommend the study of violence-positive materials, 13% of the adult males worshipers wore beards; 15% wore religious hats; and 87% wore Western garb.

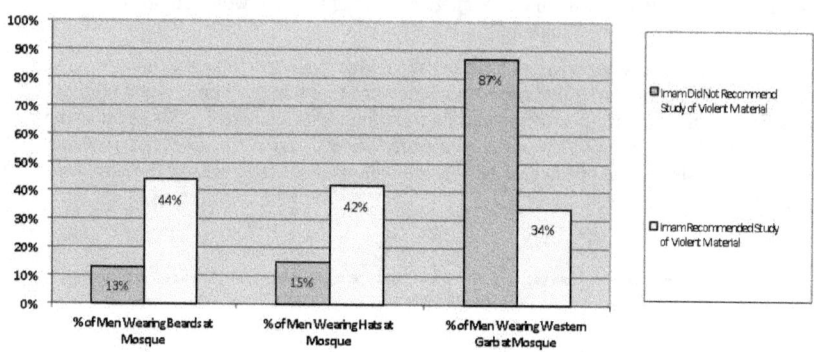

Association of Adult Male Worshiper Characteristics and Whether the Imams Recommended the Study of Violence-Positive Materials

Measures of *Sharia* adherence by non-adult male worshipers that failed to show either a relationship or a statistically significant relationship between the behavior and the presence of violence-positive materials on premises were: (a) the percentage of women with the modern hijab (as opposed to the traditional hijab or the niqab); (b) the percentage of girls with the hijab; and (b) the percentage of boys with a head covering. In mosques with no violence-positive materials, 57% of the women wore the modern hijab. Thirty-eight percent (38%) of the women wore the modern hijab in mosques that contained moderate materials; and 42% of the women wore the modern hijab in mosques that contained severe materials.

Twenty-nine percent (29%) of the girls in attendance at mosques that contained no violence-positive materials wore the hijab. Fourteen percent (14%) of the girls at mosques that contained moderate materials wore the hijab; and 36% of the girls who attended mosques that contained severe materials wore the hijab.

Of the boys in attendance at mosques that contained no violence-positive materials, 14% wore a head covering. Twenty-four percent (24%) of the boys who attended the mosques that contained moderate materials wore a head covering; and 32% of the boys who attended the mosques that contained severe materials wore a head covering.

The percentage of women in attendance at mosque who wore a modern hijab (as opposed to the traditional hijab or the niqab) showed a statistically significant negative relationship to whether the imam would recommend the study of violence positive literature. At mosques led by imams who did not recommend the study of violence-positive materials, 70% of the women wore the non-*Sharia*-adherent modern hijab; while 41% of the women wore the modern hijab at mosques led by imams who recommended worshipers study violence-positive materials.

Both the percentage of girls who wore the hijab and the percentage of boys who wore head coverings demonstrated a statistically significant relationship with whether an imam would recommend the study of violence-positive materials. However, neither of these relationships

101

were statistically significant. Twenty percent (20%) of the girls wore a hijab at mosques that were led by an imam who did not recommend the study of violence-positive materials; and 29% of the girls wore a hijab at mosques led by an imam who recommended the study of violence-positive materials. Zero percent (0%) of the boys wore a head covering at mosques that were led by an imam who did not recommend the study of violence-positive materials; and 30% of the boys wore a head covering at mosques that were led by imams who recommended the study of violence-positive materials.

Association of Presence and Strictness of Materials Found on Mosque Premises to the Promotion of Violence and Violent Jihad

The presence of violence-positive materials on mosque premises was correlated to several indicia of whether the mosque would promote violence and violent jihad. Of the mosques that contained severe materials, 100% were led by an imam who recommended that worshipers study violent materials; 100% promoted violent jihad; 98% promoted the financial support of terror; 98% promoted the establishment of the Caliphate in the United States; 100% praised terror against the West; and 76% invited guest speakers known to have promoted violent jihad.

The observed incidences of the promotion of violence and violent jihad were not substantially different for the mosques that contained only moderate materials. Of the mosques that contained only moderate materials, 97% were led by an imam who recommended the study of violent materials; 97% promoted violent jihad; 97% promoted the financial support of terror; 97% promoted the establishment of the Caliphate in the United States; 97% praised terror against the West; and 60% invited guest speakers known to have promoted violent jihad.

Mosques that contained no violence-positive materials on their premises were substantially less likely to engage in several measures of violence- and violent-jihad-promoting behaviors than were mosques that contained such materials. Of the mosques that contained no violence-positive materials, 18% were led by an imam who recommended the study of violent materials; 5% promoted violent jihad; 5% promoted the financial support of terror; 5% promoted the establishment of the Caliphate in the United States; 5% praised terror against the West; and 5% invited guest speakers known to have promoted violent jihad.

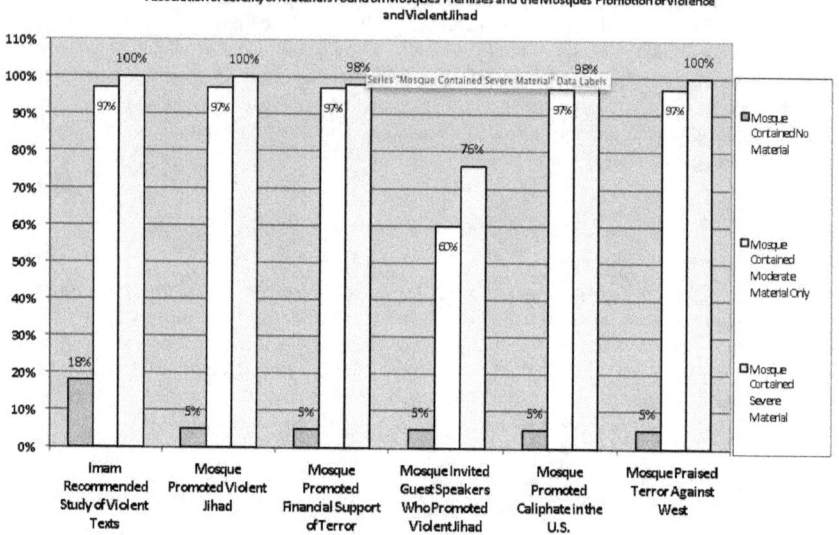

Association of Severity of Materials Found on Mosques' Premises and the Mosques' Promotion of Violence and Violent Jihad

Either no relationship existed or no statistically significant relationship existed between the presence of materials found on mosque premises and whether mosques: (a) promoted joining a terrorist organization; (b) collected money openly for a known terrorist organization; and (c) distributed memorabilia that featured jihadists or terrorist organizations. Of the mosques that contained severe materials, 10% promoted joining a terrorist organization; 8% collected money openly for known terrorist organizations; and 12% distributed memorabilia that featured jihadists or terrorist organizations.

Of the mosques that contained moderate materials, 7% promoted joining a terrorist organization; 3% collected money openly for known terrorist organizations; and 7% distributed memorabilia that featured jihadists or terrorist organizations.

Of the mosques that contained no violence-positive materials, 5% promoted joining a terrorist organization; 5% collected money openly for known terrorist organizations; and 5% distributed memorabilia that featured jihadists or terrorist organizations.

Validity of Variable Selection

While violence-positive literature was found at both mosques that manifested the more strict, orthodox *Sharia*-adherent behaviors and their non-*Sharia*-adherent counterparts, violence-positive literature was more likely to be found in those mosques whose behaviors conformed to orthodox, *Sharia*-adherent Islam. The survey results report a modest statistically significant correlation between the presence of violence-positive literature in mosques and the presence of a greater percentage of adult male worshippers who exhibit *Sharia*-adherent behavioral characteristics.

In addition to this modest correlation between *Sharia* adherence and the presence of violence-positive literature, the presence of violence-positive literature was also related to whether mosque leadership would engage in certain behaviors that are promotive of violence and violent *jihad*. Imams of mosques that contained violence-positive literature were more likely to recommend that worshippers study violence-promoting texts than were imams of mosques where no violence-positive literature was found. Additionally, mosques where violence-positive literature was present were more likely to invite guest speakers who are known to have promoted violent *jihad* than were the mosques where no violent literature was present. The fact that the imams in the *Sharia*-adherent mosques, as measured by the behavior of the worshippers, were more likely to recommend the violence-positive literature and the fact that these mosques were more likely to have invited guest speakers known to have promoted violent *jihad* further confirms the variable selection.

The authors of this survey are not asserting that there is no legitimate reason for mosques to have the surveyed texts available on mosque premises. However, the results are noteworthy precisely because this correlation with violence-positive literature combined with its promotion at *Sharia*-adherent mosques was almost non-existent in mosques typified by more assimilative behaviors.

The Role of the Sharia-Centric Mosque in Supporting the Violent Jihad

This survey serves as empirical support for anecdotal studies that have noted a connection between highly *Sharia*-adherent mosques and the recruitment of those among their respective worshippers who commit political violence in the name of Islam. [96] The mosque leadership of some highly *Sharia*-adherent mosques with known terrorist connections have praised suicide bombers and the mosques have sold literature that advocated violence against disfavored groups. [97]

This survey's results help to provide insight into the role that *Sharia*-adherent behaviors possibly play in defining group identities, creating an us-versus-them outlook, and projecting violence against outgroups such as the West and non-Muslims, which is mirrored by the *Sharia* literature found in the mosques prone to violent literature. [98] The mosques where greater indicia of *Sharia*-adherent behaviors were observed were more likely to contain materials that conveyed a positive attitude toward employing violent *jihad* against the West and non-Muslims than were mosques where more Western, assimilative behaviors were observed. These materials may be instrumental in drawing a fault line between the ingroup of devout, *Sharia*-adherent Muslims and the outgroup comprised of non-Muslims and those Muslims who embrace Western values.

The fact that "spiritual sanctioners" who help individuals become progressively more radicalized are known to be connected to highly *Sharia*-adherent mosques [99] is another concern in addition to the presence of violence-positive texts at these mosques. The imams at *Sharia*-adherent mosques are far more likely to recommend that their worshippers study materials that promote violence. A recommendation from a respected religious leader that a worshipper study violence-promoting legal and normative literature may legitimatize the material's message that it is acceptable to use violence against outgroup members. Additionally, receiving permission from a religious leader to immerse oneself in materials that promote violence against outgroup members may serve as tacit permission to employ violence against an outgroup.

Mosques where greater indicia of *Sharia*-adherent behaviors are observed also manifest behaviors that are at least sympathetic to violent *jihad* and those who commit violent *jihad*. Mosques where the greatest indicia of *Sharia*-adherent behaviors were observed were the mosques most likely to contain materials holding positive views of violent *jihad*. In almost every instance, the imams at these mosques where violence-positive materials were available recommended that worshippers at their mosques study texts that promote violence. These same highly *Sharia*-adherent mosques where violence-positive materials were present—almost without exception—engaged in activities that promoted violent *jihad* and were several times more likely to invite guest preachers who were known to have supported violent *jihad* than were mosques in which violence-positive materials were not available.

Non-Sharia-Centricism and "Reform" Islam

The authors recognize—and the survey demonstrates—that there are mosques and mosque-going Muslims who are interested in a non-*Sharia*-centric Islam where tolerance of the other, rather than hatred of the other, at least as evidenced by the absence of violence-positive and *jihad*-promoting literature is the norm. The survey helps to confirm previous anecdotal [100] and less rigorous empirical efforts [101] that have observed that a majority of the mosques in the U.S. have been inundated with Salafist violent literature and Saudi-trained imams and that only a minority of mosques eschew all forms of violent literature and dogma. These exceptional mosques where violence-positive literature were not recommended exhibited significantly fewer indicia of orthodox, *Sharia*-adherent behaviors than those mosques where such literature was recommended for study and were also significantly less likely to promote violent *jihad* or invite speakers known to have promoted violent *jihad* than mosques that were typified by *Sharia*-adherent behaviors.

Discussion of the Broader Policy Implications

Prior Surveys and the Search for Predictive Variables

Recent polling surveys of several predominantly Muslim countries present a picture of a global Muslim community that is in conflict about support for employing violence against civilians and the groups who commit violence against civilians. On the one hand, an April 2007 survey by WorldPublicOpinion.org revealed that majorities in Morocco (57%), Egypt (77%), Pakistan (81%), and Indonesia (84%) believe that attacks on civilians designed to achieve political goals are never justified. [102] Strong majorities in these countries, except for Pakistan, believe groups that employ violence against civilians do so in contradiction to Islamic tenets. Strikingly, in Pakistan, only 30% of the respondents agree with the proposition that groups violate Islamic principles when they employ violence against civilians. However, 66% of Moroccans agreed with the proposition; as did 88% of Egyptians; and 65% of Indonesians. [103] It is noteworthy that the survey questionnaire did not make it clear whether the target civilians were Muslims or non-Muslims.

While support for political violence in the survey was a mixed bag, the survey did find that majorities in each country favored (a) strict application of *Sharia* law in every Islamic country and (b) keeping Western values out of Islamic counties. Both of these attitudes are consistent with the goals of Al Qaeda and were understood as aligned with Al Qaeda by the respondents: [104]

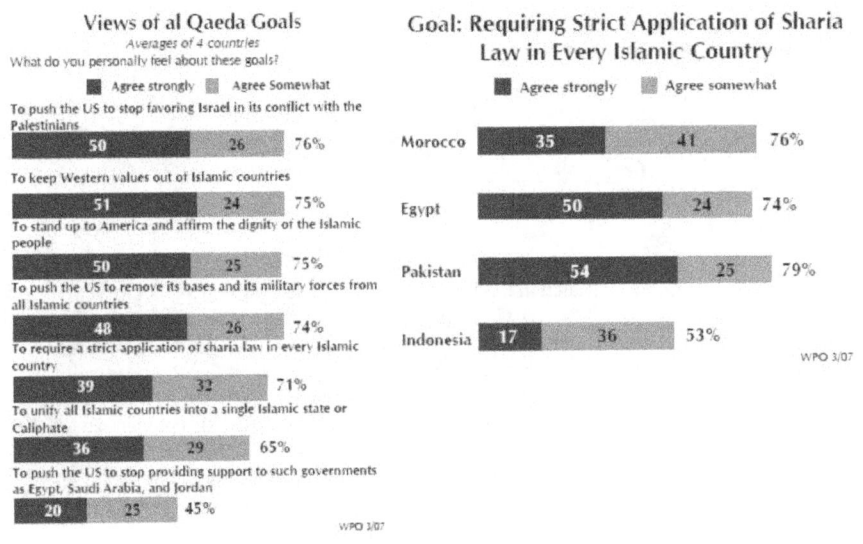

These survey results appear to be supported by a more recent 2010 Pew Survey, which surveyed Muslims in Indonesia, Egypt, Nigeria, Jordan, Pakistan, Lebanon, and Turkey. The Pew Survey found that very large majorities in each of these countries (except Turkey) support a dominant role for Islam in politics. [105] Even more significantly, large segments of the populations in these countries favor *Sharia* criminal punishments, including capital punishment for those who choose to leave Islam (i.e., apostasy). [106]

Views of Harsh Punishments

% Favor

	Stoning people who commit adultery	Whippings/cutting off of hands for theft and robbery	Death penalty for people who leave the Muslim religion
	%	%	%
Turkey	16	13	5
Egypt	82	77	84
Jordan	70	58	86
Lebanon	23	13	6
Indonesia	42	36	30
Pakistan	82	82	76
Nigeria	56	65	51

Asked of Muslims only.

PEW RESEARCH CENTER Q108b-d.

A recent study by Andrew F. March in the field of political theory pursued an inquiry into whether Islamic doctrine would allow Muslims to cooperate socially with non-Muslims and sincerely affirm liberal citizenship, as that term is understood in its Western democratic sense. March found grounds for an overlapping consensus based on a study of the *Quran* as well as works by some contemporary Muslim jurists and exegetes, but he also noted that there exists contemporary and prominent *Sharia* scholars who cite to authoritative texts holding that Muslims are either at war with non-Muslims or, at best, are in a state devoid of any obligation to socially cooperate with non-Muslims. [107] Additionally, March noted that the underpinnings of his theoretical overlapping consensus might in fact be negated by empirical evidence showing that a large percentage of Muslims were unaware of [or reject] the theological or philosophical arguments that militate toward a moral affirmation of liberal citizenship. [108]

The results of both the World Public Opinion Survey and the Pew 2010 Survey suggest that there are large segments of the Muslim world, representing demographics which rival the West, that reject quite emphatically the notion of liberal citizenship, freedom of worship, and other political mores taken for granted in the West. These surveys, however, report the attitudes of residents in non-Western countries which enforce *Sharia* to varying degrees. We might expect Muslims in the West—who are immersed in Western culture, values, and representative government—to express different attitudes than their counterparts in the Middle East, Far East, and North Africa.

Unfortunately, the results of this survey suggests that Islam—at least as it is generally practiced in mosques across the United States—continues to manifest a resistance to a sufficiently tolerant religio-legal framework that would allow its followers to make a sincere affirmation of Western citizenship. This survey provides empirical support for the view that mosques across the U.S., as institutional and social settings for mosque-going Muslims, provide a milieu resistant to, the legal, theological, or political arguments that make political, civic, and social cooperation within a secular constitutional political order ideal.

This Survey's Limitations

This survey only examined the presence of *Sharia*-adherent behaviors, the presence of violence-positive materials in mosques, whether an imam would promote the study of violence-positive materials, and whether an imam would use his mosque as forum to promote violent *jihad*. The authors note that most of the content of the texts used to rank strictness of dogma and violence in the moderate category of violence in the cause of *Sharia* includes material that does not relate to these topics and incorporates a host of other theological matters. This survey sampling of mosques also has several limitations. Since there is no central body to which all mosques belong, it was difficult to be certain that our sampling universe list was complete. Additionally, despite our preparatory efforts, many mosques were no longer at their address of record. This may have introduced bias into our sampling, although we found no evidence of any systemic distortions.

Further, the results of this survey do not tell us the percentage of American Muslims that actually attend mosques with any regularity, or at all, nor does it tell us what relative percentage of all American Muslims present as *Sharia*-adherent and non-*Sharia*-adherent. Moreover, although this study captured whether imams at highly *Sharia*-adherent mosques would recommend studying violence-positive materials and would utilize their mosques for behaviors supportive of violent *jihad*, the survey did not capture the individual mosque attendees' attitudes toward violence and violent *jihad*. It is reasonable to conclude, the authors believe, that the worshippers at the more *Sharia*-adherent mosques, where the imam is more likely to promote the violent literature and *jihad* generally, are more inclined to be sympathetic to the message conveyed in the violent and *jihad* literature than their counterparts who attend the lesser *Sharia*-adherent mosques where the material is either not present or the imam does not promote it. A follow-up survey of individual mosque attendees would provide better insight regarding the relationship, if any, between *Sharia*-adherence on the individual or mosque level and an individual's attitude toward violence and violent *jihad*.

About the authors:

Dr. Mordechai Kedar *served for 25 years in Israel's Military Intelligence specialising in Arab political discourse and mass media and Islamic groups. He is an assistant professor in the Department of Arabic and Middle East Studies at Bar-Ilan U. since 1994.*

David Yerushalmi *is a lawyer specializing in litigation and public policy research, especially relating to geo-strategic policy and national security. As general counsel to the Center for Security Policy, he focuses his professional work on Islamic law and its intersection with Islamic terrorism and national security.*

The authors and the editors of Perspectives on Terrorism wish to acknowledge and express gratitude to the *Middle East Quarterly*, which originally published the results of this study in its Summer 2011 edition (available online at http://www.meforum.org/2931/american-mosques) for granting permission to republish the results of this study in a more expansive online format.

Notes:

[1] These survey results were first published in "Shari'a and Violence in American Mosques," Middle East Quarterly, Summer 2011, pp. 59-72, available at http://www.meforum.org/2931/american-mosques. The authors would like to acknowledge the Center for Security Policy for its funding the largest portion of the survey costs. The authors would also like to acknowledge Professor Jonathan Rabinowitz, of Bar-Ilan University's Louis and Gabi Weisfeld School of Social Work, for his assistance in data and statistical analysis, and Pete Rowe, Esq., for his invaluable and dedicated contribution in finalizing this article for publication.

[2] See Marc Sageman, Understanding Terror Networks (University of Pennsylvania Press 2004) and James A. Piazza, *Rooted in Poverty?: Terrorism, Poor Economic Development, and Social Cleavages*, 18 Terrorism and Political Violence 159, 159-77 (2006).
[3] Marc Sageman, *Understanding Terror Networks* 73-74 (University of Pennsylvania Press 2004) and James A. Piazza, *Rooted in Poverty?: Terrorism, Poor Economic Development, and Social Cleavages*, 18 Terrorism and Political Violence 159, 170-71 (2006).
[4] Paul Gill, *A Multi-Dimensional Approach to Suicide Bombing*, 1(2) International Journal of Conflict and Violence 142, 142-59 (2007).
[5] Id. at 157.
[6] See id. at 142-159.
[7] Marc Sageman, *Understanding Terror Networks* 93 (University of Pennsylvania Press, 2004).
[8] Id.
[9] See Mitchell D. Silber & Arvin Bhatt, *Radicalization in the West: The Homegrown Threat* (New York City Police Department 2007).
[10] See Id.
[11] Sageman, *supra* note 1, at 63.
[12] Id. at 115.
[13] Id. at 143-44.
[14] Susan Sachs, *A Muslim Missionary Group Draws New Scrutiny in U.S.*, N.Y. Times, July 14, 2003, and avail. at http://www.hvk.org/articles/0703/113.html, accessed December 8, 2010 (discussing the *Tablighi Jamaat* practice of setting up residence by sleeping in mosques and the Tablighi Jamaat connection to American Taliban John Walker Lindh) and Salah Uddin Shoaib Choudhury, *Tablighi Jamaat—Preaching Jihad*, American Chronicle, Oct. 14, 2009, and avail. at http://www.americanchronicle.com/articles/view/123722, accessed December 8, 2010 (discussing the *Tablighi Jamaat* connection with members of an Oregon cell that plotted to blow up synagogues, Lyman Harris, who planned to blow up the Brooklyn Bridge, and Jose Padilla, who planned to set off a 'dirty bomb' in an American city).
[15] Silber and Bhatt, *supra* note 8, at 38.
[16] Id. at 10, 38.
[17] See id. at 41-42 (discussing the role of "spiritual sanctioners" Imam Abdul Nacer Benbrinka in the Melborne and Sydney, Australia terror cells and Qayyum Abdul Jamaal in the Toronto, Canada terror cell) and Ethan Sacks, *Who is Anwar al-Awlaki? Imam Contacted by Fort Hood Gunman has Long Radical Past*, N.Y. Daily News, Nov. 11, 2009, and avail. at http://www.nydailynews.com/news/national/2009/11/11/2009-11-11_who_is_anwar_alawlaki_imam_contacted_by_fort_hood_gunman_nidal_malik_hasan_has_l.html, accessed January 2, 2011 (discussing Anwar Al Awalki's connections to several 9/11 hijackers and accused Fort Hood terrorist, Nidal Malik Hassan).
[18] Silber and Bhatt, *supra* note 8, at 38.
[19] See Quintan Wiktorowicz, *A Genealogy of Radical Islam*, 28 Studies in Conflict and Terrorism 75, 75-97 (2005).
[20] Id. at 76-77.
[21] Id. at 90.
[22] Martin Harrow, *The Complexity of Transnational Islamist Militancy: Why Islamist Militancy Causes Islamist Militancy*, Paper Presented at ISA Conference: Complexity Science in International Relations, San Francisco, California (March 25, 2008).
[23] See Sageman, *supra* note 1 and Piazza, *supra* note 1.
[24] Jeremy Gingea, et al., *Religion and Support for Suicide Attacks*, 20(2) Psychology Science 224, 224-30 (2009).
[25] Id.
[26] Id.
[27] Id. at 230.
[28] Id.
[29] Saba Mahmood, *Rehearsed Spontaneity and the Conventionality of Ritual: Disciplines of Salat*, 28(4) American Ethnologist 827, 830(Nov. 2004).
[30] Daniel Winchester, *Embodying the Faith: Religious Practice and the Making of Muslim Moral Habitus*, 4(86) Social Forces 1753, 1765 (June 2008) and 2 Sayid Sabiq, Fiqh-us-Sunnah English Transl. 67-74 (American Trust Publications 1991).
[31] Ginges et al., *supra* note 24, at 225-26.
[32] Id.
[33] Azman Ismail, *Sharia Framework for Takaful* 1, avail. at http://www.takaful.coop/doc_store/takaful/Shariah%20Framework%20of%20Takaful.pdf, accessed Nov. 1, 2010.
[34] Azman Ismail, *Sharia Framework for Takaful*, avail. at http://www.takaful.coop/doc_store/takaful/Shariah%20Framework%20of%20Takaful.pdf, accessed Nov. 1, 2010.

[35] GlobalSecurity.org, *Sunni Islam*, avail. at *http://www.globalsecurity.org/military/intro/islam-sunni.htm* accessed Nov. 1, 2010.
[36] Joseph Schacht, *An Introduction to Islamic Law* 68 at fn.1 (Oxford University Press 1982).
[37] 1 Choucri Cardahi, *Law in the Middle East* 341-42 (The Middle East Institute 1955).
[38] The Royal Aal Al-Bayt Institute for Islamic Thought, *The Three Points of the Amman Message (2007)*, avail. at *http://ammanmessage.com/index.php?option=com_content&task=view&id=91&Itemid=74*, accessed Nov. 21, 2010.
[39] The Royal Aal Al-Bayt Institute for Islamic Thought, *Jihad and the Islamic Law of War* 57 (2007), and avail. at *http://ammanmessage.com/media/jihad.pdf*, last accessed Nov. 6, 2010.
[40] Wael B. Hallaq, *Shari'a: Theory, Practice, Transformations*, 72-78 (Cambridge University Press 2009).
[41] James Thornback, *The Portrayal of Sharia in Ontario*, 10(1) Appeal: Review of Current Law and Law Reform (citing to D.S. El Alami & D. Hinchcliffe, *Islamic Marriage and Divorce Laws of the Arab World* 3 (Klewer Law International 1996).
[42] *Id.* (citing to D.S. El Alami & D. Hinchcliffe, *Islamic Marriage and Divorce Laws of the Arab World* 3 (Klewer Law International 1996)).
[43] Ahmad Ibn Naqib Al-Misri, *Reliance of the Traveller and Tools for the Worshipper* vii-Introduction (Sheikh Nuh Ha Mim Keller trans., 1991) and avail. at http://www.shafiifiqh.com/maktabah/relianceoftraveller.pdf, accessed Nov. 21, 2010.
[44] Sheyk al-Akbar Mahmud Shaltut, Head of the al-Azhar University, Fatwa Announced July 6, 1959 and avail. at http://www.freewebs.com/islamic-site/pic/azhar.jpg, accessed Nov. 6, 2010.
[45] The Royal Al-Bayt Institute for Islamic Thought, *The Amman Message* 16-18 (2007) and avail. at *http://ammanmessage.com/media/Amman-Message-pdf-booklet-v-2-5-2-08.pdf*, accessed Nov. 6, 2010.
[46] Wael B. Hallaq, *Shari'a: Theory, Practice, Transformations* 113-24 (Cambridge University Press 2009).
[47] *Id.* at 72-78.
[48] Sageman, *supra* note 1, at 1.
[49] The Royal Aal Al-Bayt Institute for Islamic Thought, *supra*, note 39, at 60.
[50] *Id.*
[51] Sageman, *supra* note 1, at 2.
[52] Andrew F. March, *Islam and Liberal Citizenship: The Search for an Overlapping Consensus* 116 (Oxford University Press 2009) and *See* Sageman, *supra* note 1, at 2.
[53] March, *supra* note 52, at 117 and Sageman, *supra* note 1, at 2.
[54] March, *supra* note 52, at 117 and Sageman, *supra* note 1, at 2.
[55] March, *supra* note 52, at 119.
[56] The Royal Aal Al-Bayt Institute for Islamic Thought, *supra* note 39, at 64-66.
[57] *Id.* at 66.
[58] *See e.g.* 1 Hafiz Ibn Kathir, *Tafsir Ibn Kathir* Abridged, 596 (Darussalam Publishers 2000); 3 Hafiz Ibn Kathir, *Tafsir Ibn Kathir* Abridged, 170 (Darussalam Publishers 2000); and 4 Hafiz Ibn Kathir, *Tafsir Ibn Kathir* Abridged, 376 (Darussalam Publishers 2000).
[59] *See* David Yerushalmi, *Selected Classical Sources on Jihad (Law Offices of David Yerushalmi 2009)*, and avail. at *http://www.saneworks.us/uploads/application/52.pdf*, accessed Nov. 6, 2010.
[60] *Id.* at 2-3.
[61] *Id.* at 1-2.
[62] Mary Habeck, *Knowing the Enemy: Jihadist Ideology and the War on Terror*, 116 (Yale Univ. Press 2006).
[63] Al Azhar University, *Certification of Reliance of the Traveller* (1991). and avail. at http://www.exmuslim.org/Certificate%20Al-Azhar%20Reliance%20of%20the%20Traveller.pdf, accessed Nov. 7, 2010.
[64] David Yerushalmi, *supra* note 59, at 6.
[65] Amir Taheri, Holy Terror: Inside the World of Islamic Terrorism 242-43 (Adler & Adler 1987).
[66] Barry A. Kosmin &Seymour P. Lachman, *One Nation Under God: Religion in Contemporary American Society* (Harmony Books 1993).
[67] *See* at 96-97, 286 (Due to the margin of error of +/- 0.2% in the Muslim population statistics, we included South Carolina with a 0.97% Muslim population. The District of Columbia was added because of the sizable Muslim populations in Maryland and Virginia that work in the District and thus pray in mosques located in the District and near their places of work).
[68] Ihsan Bagby et al., *The Mosque in America: A National Portrait* (2001), and avail. at http://sun.cair.com/Portals/0/pdf/The_Mosque_in_America_A_National_Portrait.pdf, accessed Oct. 30, 2010.
[69] Harvard University, *Pluralism Project*, avail. at http://pluralism.org/directory/index/country:US/state.all/tradition:9, accessed Oct. 30, 2010.
[70] *See* Appendix A for a complete explanation of the behaviors that were scored as Sharia adherent, the materials that were scored as violence positive, and the behaviors that were scored as promoting violence or violent jihad.
[71] *Id.*
[72] 1 Sayid Sabiq, *Fiqh-us-Sunnah* English Transl., 113 (American Trust Publications 1991).
[73] Al-Misri, *supra* note 43, at F5.3.
[74] *Id.* at F5.6.
[75] Al-Misri, *supra* note 43, at F12.4 and, 2 Sayid Sabiq, *Fiqh-us-Sunnah* English Transl., 50, 56 (American Trust Publications 1991).
[76] *Id.* at F12.32 and *see* Sabiq, *supra* note 73, at 64a.
[77] Al-Misri, *supra* note 43, at F8.2 and Sabiq, *supra* note 73, at 50,56.
[78] The Royal Aal Al-Bayt Institute for Islamic Thought, *supra* note 39, at 58.
[79] *Id.* at 58-59.
[80] *Id.* at 59.
[81] *Id.* at 59.
[82] *Id.*
[83] *Id.* at 60.
[84] *Id.* at 59.
[85] Al-Misri, *supra* note 43, at O9.8.
[86] *Id.* at O9.9.
[87] Sabiq, *supra* note 70, at 77b.
[88] 4 Hafiz Ibn Kathir, *Tafsir Ibn Kathir* Abridged, 475 (Darussalam Publishers 2000).
[89] Sageman, *supra* note 1, at 6-7.

[90] Abul A'la Maududi, *Jihad in Islam*, and avail. at *http://www.muhammadanism.org/Terrorism/jihad_in_islam/jihad_in_islam.pdf*, accessed Nov. 26, 2010.

[91] Sageman, *supra* note 1, at 9.

[92] Sayyid Qutb, *Milestones* 34, and avail. at *http://majalla.org/books/2005/qutb-milestone.pdf*, accessed Nov. 26, 2010.

[93] Sageman, *supra* note 1, at 9.

[94] 3 Sayid Sabiq, *Fiqh-us-Sunnah* 76 (American Trust Publications 1991).

[95] See Appendix B to view the tables containing the data referenced in both the Results discussion and the graphs embedded within the Results discussion.

[96] *See* Silber and Bhatt, *supra* note 8.

[97] *Id.* at 33.

[98] *See* Appendix A for excerpts from the Sharia literature found in those mosques that made available materials supportive of violence.

[99] Silber and Bhatt, *supra* note 8, at 35 and Sacks, *supra* note 16 (discussing Anwar Al Awalki's connections to several 9/11 hijackers and accused Fort Hood terrorist, Nidal Malik Hassan).

[100] *See, e.g.,* Shaykh Muhammad Hisham Kabbani, *Islamic Extremism: A Viable Threat to U.S. National Security*, presentation delivered at Open Forum at the U.S. Department of State, January 7, 1999 and avail. at http://members.fortunecity.com/amimm/Extremism.html, accessed March 23, 2011; see also Kabbani, *The Muslim Experience in America is Unprecedented*, 7(2) Middle East Qtrly, June 2000, at 6-7 and avail. at http://www.meforum.org/61/muhammad-hisham-kabbani-the-muslim-experience-in, accessed March 23, 2011.

[101] *See, e.g.,* Center for Religious Freedom & Freedom House, *Saudi Publications on Hate Ideology Invade American Mosques* (2005) and avail. at http://www.freedomhouse.org/uploads/special_report/45.pdf, accessed March 23, 2011.

[102] WorldPublicOpinion.org, The Program on International Policy Attitudes at the University of Maryland, *Muslim Public Opinion on U.S. Policy, Attacks on Civilians, and Al Qaeda* (April 24, 2007), pp. 9-10.

[103] *Id.*, p. 10.

[104] *Id.* at 15, 21-22.

[105] Pew Research Center, Global Attitudes Project, *Muslim Publics Divided on Hamas and Hezbollah*, pp. 10-11.

[106] *Id.*, p. 14.

[107] March, *supra* note 52, at 266.

[108] *Id.* at 274.

Appendix A: Excerpts from violent materials made available in mosques

Source Document	Page Number/ Location	Subject Matter	Excerpt*
*Parentheses used in the excerpted material also appeared in the original source documents. The authors used brackets when making comments to offer clarity or context in the excerpted material.			
Fiqh-us-Sunnah	Vol. 1, Page 77b	Apostates	Ibn 'Abbas reported that the Prophet, upon whom be peace, said, "The ties of Islam and the principles of the religion are three, and whoever leaves one of them becomes an unbeliever, and his blood becomes lawful: testifying that there is no god except Allah, the obligatory prayers, and the fast of Ramadan." (Related by Abu Ya'la with a hassan chain.) Another narration states, "If anyone leaves one of them, by Allah he becomes an unbeliever and no voluntary deeds or recompense will be accepted from him, and his blood and wealth become lawful." This is a clear indication that such a person is to be killed.
Fiqh-us-Sunnah	Vol. 1, Page 77b	Non-muslims	Ibn 'Umar related that the Messenger of Allah, upon whom be peace, said, "I have been ordered to kill the people until they testify that there is no god except Allah, and that Muhammad is the Messenger of Allah, and they establish prayer and pay the zakah. If they do that, their blood and wealth are protected from me save by the rights of Islam. Their reckoning will be with Allah."
Fiqh-us-Sunnah	Vol. 1, Page 77b	Apostates	Says ash-Shaukani, "The truth of the matter is that he becomes an unbeliever who is to be killed for his unbelief. The hadith authenticates that Islamic law calls one who does not pray an unbeliever. It has also put the performance as the barrier between a believer and an unbeliever. Abandoning prayer means he may be called an unbeliever.
Fiqh-us-Sunnah	Vol 1. Page 80	Children	Although it is not obligatory for a child to pray, it is a must that his guardian order him to do so when he is seven, and he should beat him if he does not pray after he reaches the age of ten. A minor should practice praying until he reaches puberty. 'Amr ibn Shu'aib related from his father on the authority of his grandfather that the Prophet, peace be upon him, said, "Order your children to pray when they reach the age of seven. Beat them (if they don't pray) when they reach the age of ten. And have them sleep separately."
Fiqh-us-Sunnah	Vol. 1, Page 113	Women/Hijab	There is no such dispute over what constitutes a woman's 'aurah [private parts/nakedness]. It is stated that her entire body is 'aurah and must be covered, except her hands and face. Says Allah in the Qur'an, "And to display of their adornment only that which is apparent (do not expose any adornment or beauty save the hands and face)." It has been authentically related from Ibn 'Abbas, Ibn 'Umar and 'Aishah that the Prophet said, "Allah does not accept the prayer of an adult woman unless she is wearing a headcovering (khimar, hijab)." This is related by "the five," except for an-Nasa'i, and by Ibn Khuzaimah and al-Hakim. At-Tirmizhi grades it as hassan.

Source Document	Page Number/ Location	Subject Matter	Excerpt*
Fiqh-us-Sunnah	Vol.2, Page 50 & 56	Women/Prayer	As stated earlier, it is better for women to pray in their houses. Ahmad and at-Tabarani record that Umm Humaid as-Sa'diyah came to the Messenger of Allah and said: "O Messenger of Allah, I love to pray with you." The Prophet said: "I am aware of that, but your salah in your residence is better for you than your salah in your people's mosque. And your salah in your people's mosque is better than your salah in the [larger] congregational Mosque."
Fiqh-us-Sunnah	Vol. 2, Page 62b	Women/Prayer	If a woman is present with the group, then she is to stand in a row by herself behind the men and she is not to join them in their rows. If she did not stand in a separate row, her salah will still be valid according to the opinion of majority. Anas said: "An orphan and I prayed behind the Messenger of Allah in our house and my mother prayed behind us." In another version it is stated: "He put me and the orphan in a row behind him and the woman behind us." This is related by al-Bukhari and Muslim.
Fiqh-us-Sunnah	Vol. 2, Page 64a	Prayer Lines	"It is preferred for the imam to order the followers to straighten the rows and fill in any gaps before he starts the salah. Anas relates: ""The Prophet would turn his face to us before he began the salah and he would say: 'Be close together and straighten your rows.""" This is related by al-Bukhari and Muslim. He also reported that the Prophet would say: ""Make your rows straight for the straightening of the rows is part of the completion of the salah."""
Fiqh-us-Sunnah	Vol. 3, Page 7	Apostates	Abu Hurairah is reported to have said: "When Allah's Messenger, upon whom be peace, died and Abu Bakr succeeded him as caliph, some Arabs apostasized, causing Abu Bakr to declare war upon them. 'Umar said to him: 'Why must you fight these men?', especially when there is a ruling of the Prophet, upon whom be peace: 'I have been called to fight men until they say that none has the right to be worshipped but Allah, and whoever said it has saved his life and property from me except when a right is due in them, and his account will be with Allah.' Abu Bakr replied: 'By Allah! I will fight those who differentiate between salah and zakah because zakah is the due on property. By Allah! If they withheld even a young she-goat ('anaq) that they used to pay at the time of Allah's Messenger, upon whom be peace, I would fight them.' Then 'Umar said: 'By Allah! It was He who gave Abu Bakr the true knowledge to fight, and later I came to know that he was right.' "

Source Document	Page Number/ Location	Subject Matter	Excerpt*
Fiqh-us-Sunnah	Vol. 3, Page 65	Non-Muslims	The Hanafiyyah say that the share [monies paid] of such people [non-Muslims] are cancelled when Islam is strong. For instance, 'Uyainah ibn Hisn, al-Aqra' ibn Habis, and al-'Abbas ibn Mirdas came to Abu Bakr and requested their share. He wrote them a letter, which they took to 'Umar. He tore the letter and said: "This is something that the Prophet, upon whom be peace, used to give you to reconcile you to Islam. Now, Allah has fortified Islam and it is no longer in need of you. Unless you stay with Islam, the sword will be between you and us. Say: 'It is the truth from the Lord of you [all]. Then whoever will, let him believe, and whoever will, let him disbelieve' [al Kahf 29]."
Fiqh-us-Sunnah	Vol. 5, Page 19	Women	Fear Allah concerning women! Verily you have taken them on the security of Allah, and intercourse with them has been made lawful unto you by word of Allah. You too have rights over them, in that they should not allow anyone to sit on your bed whom you do not like. But if they do that, you can chastise them but not severely.
Reliance of the Traveller	f1.2	Children	When a child with discrimination (O: meaning he can eat, drink, and clean himself after using the toilet unassisted) is seven years of age, he is ordered to perform the prayer, and when ten, is beaten for neglecting it (N: not severely, but so as to discipline the child, and not more than three blows).
Reliance of the Traveller	f1.3	Apostates	"Someone raised among Muslims who denies the obligatoriness of the prayer, zakat, fasting Ramadan, the pilgrimage, or the unlawfulness of wine and adultery, or denies something else upon which there is scholarly consensus (ijma', def.b7) and which is necessarily known as being of the religion (N: necessarily known meaning things that any Muslim would know about if asked) thereby becomes an unbeliever (kafir) and is executed for his unbelief (O: if he does not admit he is mistaken and acknowledge the Obligatoriness or unlawfulness of that which there is scholarly consensus upon. As for if he denies the obligatoriness of something there is not consensus upon, then he is not adjudged an unbeliever)."
Reliance of the Traveller	f1.4	Negligent Muslims	A Muslim who holds the prayer to be obligatory but through lack of concern neglects to perform it until its proper time is over has not committed unbelief (dis: w18.2). Rather, he is executed, washed, prayed over, and buried in the Muslim's cemetery (O: as he is one of them. It is recommended, but not obligatory, that he be asked to repent (N: and if he does, he is not executed)).
Reliance of the Traveller	f.5.3	Women/Hijab	The nakedness of a woman (O: even if a young girl) consists of the whole body except the face and hands. (N: The nakedness of woman is that which invalidates the prayer if exposed (dis:w23).
Reliance of the Traveller	f.5.6	Women/Hijab	It is recommended for a woman to wear a covering over her head (khimar), a full length shift, and a heavy slip under it that does not cling to the body.

Source Document	Page Number/ Location	Subject Matter	Excerpt*
Reliance of the Traveller	f8.2	Prayer Lines	"It is recommended: (1) to stand for the prayer after the end of the call to commence (iqama); (2) to be in the first row; (3) to make the rows straight, especially if one is the imam (O: when one should order the group to do so); (4) and to fill up the first row first, then the second, and so on (O: meaning there should not be a second row when the first one is not full (A: as to pray in such a second row is the same as not praying with a group, and is rewarded as if one had prayed alone), nor gaps within one row, nor a distance in excess of a meter and a half between rows). It is superior to stand on the imam's right (A: though the sunna is for the imam to be in the middle) (N: and if one arrives at a group prayer in which the row extends to the right, one's rewards is greater for standing on the left, since one is performing the sunna)."
Reliance of the Traveller	m10.11	Women	"If the wife does not fulfill one of the above-mentioned obligations, she is termed ''rebellious''(nashiz), and the husband takes the following steps to correct matters: (a) admonition and advice, by explaining the unlawfulness of rebellion, its harmful effect on married life, and by listening to her viewpoint on the matter; (b) if admonition is ineffectual, he keeps from her by not sleeping in bed with her, by which both learn the degree to which they need each other; (c) if keeping from her is ineffectual, it is permissible for him to hit her [if] he believes that hitting her will bring her back to the right path, though if he does not think so, it is not permissible. His hitting her may not be in a way that injures her, and is his last recourse to save the family; (d) if the disagreement does not end after all this, each partner chooses an arbitrator to solve the dispute by settlement, or divorce.)"
Reliance of the Traveller	o1.2	Non-muslims	The following are not subject to retaliation: ... (2) a Muslim for killing a non-Muslim;
Reliance of the Traveller	o1.2	Apostates	The following are not subject to retaliation: ... (3) a Jewish or Christian subject of the Islamic state for killing an apostate from Islam (O: because a subject of the state is under its protection, while killing an apostate from Islam is without consequences);
Reliance of the Traveller	o8.1	Apostates	When a person who has reached puberty and is sane voluntarily apostatizes from Islam, he deserves to be killed.
Reliance of the Traveller	o8.2	Apostates	In such a case, it is obligatory for the caliph (A: or his representive) to ask him to repent and return to Islam. If he does, it is accepted from him, but if he refuses, he is immediately killed.

Source Document	Page Number/ Location	Subject Matter	Excerpt*
Reliance of the Traveller	o9.8	Jihad	The caliph (o25) makes war upon Jews, Christians, and Zoroastrians (N: provided he has first invited them to enter Islam in faith and practice, and if they will not, then invited them to enter the social order of Islam by paying the non-Muslim poll tax (jizya, def: o11.4)-which is the significance of their paying it, not the money itself-while remaining in their ancestral religions) (O: and the war continues) until they become Muslim or else pay the non-Muslim poll tax (O: in accordance with the word of Allah Most High, "Fight those who do not believe in Allah and the Last Day and who forbid not what Allah and His messenger have forbidden-who do not practice the religion of truth, being of those who have been given the Book-until they pay the poll tax out of hand and are humbled" (Koran 9.29)
Reliance of the Traveller	o9.9	Jihad	The caliph fights all other peoples until they become Muslim (O: because they are not a people with a Book, nor honored as such, and are not permitted to settle with paying the poll tax (jizya))
Reliance of the Traveller	o10.1	Jihad	A free male Muslim who has reached puberty and is sane is entitled to the spoils of battle when he has participated in a battle to the end of it.
Reliance of the Traveller	o10.2	Jihad	As for personal booty, anyone who, despite resistance, kills one of the enemy or effectively incapacitates him, risking his own life thereby, is entitled to whatever he can take from the enemy, meaning as much as he can take away with him in the battle, such as a mount, clothes, weaponry, money, or other.
Reliance of the Traveller	p42.2	Women	Allah Most High says: "Men are the guardians of women, since Allah has been more generous to one than the other, and because of what they (men) spend from their wealth. so righteous women will be obedient, and in absence watchful, for Allah is watchful. And if you fear their intractability, warn them, send them from bed, or hit them. But if they obey you, seek no way to blame them" (Koran 4:34).
Qutb's Milestones	Chapter 4	Jihad	The third kind [of non-Muslim] were those with whom there was neither a treaty nor were they fighting against the Prophet-peace be on him-, or those with whom no term of expiration was stated. Concerning these, it was commanded that they be given four months' notice of expiration, at the end of which they should be considered open enemies and fought with.
Qutb's Milestones	Chapter 4	Jihad	If someone does this [prevents others from accepting Islam], then it is the duty of Islam to fight him until either he is killed or until he declares his submission.
Qutb's Milestones	Chapter 4	Jihad	Fight against those among the People of the Book who do not believe in God and the Last Day, who do not forbid what God and His messenger have forbidden, and who do not consider the true religion as their way of life, until they are subdued and pay Jiziyah.

Source Document	Page Number/ Location	Subject Matter	Excerpt*
Qutb's Milestones	Chapter 4	Non-Muslims	"It was also explained that war should be declared against those from among the People of the Book [16 Christians and Jews] who declare open enmity, until they agree to pay Jiziyah or accept Islam."
Qutb's Milestones	Chapter 4	Non-Muslims	Concerning the polytheists and the hypocrites, it was commanded in this chapter that Jihad be declared against them and that they be treated harshly. The Prophet-peace be on him-carried on Jihad against the polytheists by fighting and against the hypocrites by preaching and argument.
Qutb's Milestones	Chapter 4	Non-Muslims	Thus, after the revelation of the chapter Bara'ah, the unbelievers were of three kinds: adversaries in war, people with treaties, and Dhimmies [second-class citizens within the Islamic state]. The people with treaties eventually became Muslims, so there were only two kinds left: people at war and Dhimmies.
Qutb's Milestones	Chapter 4	Jihad	"This group of thinkers, who are a product of the sorry state of the present Muslim generation, have nothing but the label of Islam and have laid down their spiritual and rational arms in defeat. They say, ""Islam has prescribed only defensive war""!..."
Qutb's Milestones	Chapter 4	Jihad	"When writers with defeatist and apologetic mentalities write about ""Jihad in Islam,"" trying to remove this 'blot' from Islam, then they are mixing up two things: first, that this religion forbids the imposition of its belief by force, as is clear from the verse, ""There is no compulsion in religion""(2:256), while on the other hand it tries to annihilate all those political and material powers which stand between people and Islam, which force one people to bow before another people and prevent them from accepting the sovereignty of God. These two principles have no relation to one another nor is there room to mix them. In spite of this, these defeatist-type people try to mix the two aspects and want to confine Jihad to what today is called 'defensive war'."
Qutb's Milestones	Chapter 4	Jihad	"Anyone who understands this particular character of this religion will also understand the place of Jihad bi al-sayf (striving through fighting), which is to clear the way for striving through preaching in the application of the Islamic movement. He will understand that Islam is not a defensive movement in the narrow sense which today is technically called a defensive war. This narrow meaning is ascribed to it by those who are under the pressure of circumstances and are defeated by the wily attacks of the orientalists, who distort the concept of Islamic Jihad. It was a movement to wipe out tyranny and to introduce true freedom to mankind, using resources according to the actual human situation, and it had definite stages, for each of which it utilized new methods."

Source Document	Page Number/ Location	Subject Matter	Excerpt*
Qutb's Milestones	Chapter 4	Jihad	If we insist on calling Islamic Jihad a defensive movement, then we must change the meaning of the word 'defense' and mean by it 'the defense of man' against all those elements which limit his freedom. These elements take the form of beliefs and concepts, as well as of political systems, based on economic, racial or class distinctions. When Islam first came into existence, the world was full of such systems, and the present-day Jahiliyyah also has various kinds of such systems.
Qutb's Milestones	Chapter 4	Jihad	Since the objective of the message of Islam is a decisive declaration of man's freedom, not merely on the philosophical plane but also in the actual conditions of life, it must employ Jihad. It is immaterial whether the homeland of Islam - in the true Islamic sense, Dar al-Islam - is in a condition of peace or whether it is threatened by its neighbors.
Qutb's Milestones	Chapter 4	Jihad	"With these verses from the Qur'an and with many Traditions of the Prophet -peace be on him - in praise of Jihad, and with the entire history of Islam, which is full of Jihad, the heart of every Muslim rejects that explanation of Jihad invented by those people whose minds have accepted defeat under unfavorable conditions and under the attacks on Islamic Jihad by the shrewd orientalists."
Qutb's Milestones	Chapter 4	Jihad	What kind of a man is it who, after listening to the commandment of God and the Traditions of the Prophet - peace be on him-and after reading about the events which occurred during the Islamic Jihad, still thinks that it is a temporary injunction related to transient conditions and that it is concerned only with the defense of the borders?
Qutb's Milestones	Chapter 4	Jihad	"Thus, this struggle is not a temporary phase but an eternal state - an eternal state, as truth and falsehood cannot co-exist on this earth. Whenever Islam stood up with the universal declaration that God's Lordship should be established over the entire earth and that men should become free from servitude to other men, the usurpers of God's authority on earth have struck out against it fiercely and have never tolerated it. It became incumbent upon Islam to strike back and release man throughout the earth from the grip of these usurpers. The eternal struggle for the freedom of man will continue until the religion is purified for God."
Qutb's Milestones	Chapter 4	Jihad	"The Jihad of Islam is to secure complete freedom for every man throughout the world by releasing him from servitude to other human beings so that he may serve his God, Who IS One and Who has no associates. This is in itself a sufficient reason for Jihad. These were the only reasons in the hearts of Muslim warriors. If they had been asked the question ""Why are you fighting?"" none would have answered, ""My country is in danger; I am fighting for its defense"" or ""The Persians and the Romans have come upon us"", or, ""We want to extend our dominion and want more spoils.""

Source Document	Page Number/ Location	Subject Matter	Excerpt*
Qutb's Milestones	Chapter 4	Jihad	"Those who say that Islamic Jihad was merely for the defense of the 'homeland of Islam' diminish the greatness of the Islamic way of life and consider it less important than their 'homeland'."
Qutb's Milestones	Chapter 4	Jihad	"We ought not to be deceived or embarrassed by the attacks of the orientalists on the origin of Jihad, nor lose self-confidence under the pressure of present conditions and the weight of the great powers of the world to such an extent that we try to find reasons for Islamic Jihad outside the nature of this religion, and try to show that it was a defensive measure under temporary conditions. The need for Jihad remains, and will continue to remain, whether these conditions exist or not!"
Qutb's Milestones	Chapter 4	Jihad	Jihad in Islam is simply a name for striving to make this system of life [Islam] dominant in the world.
Qutb's Milestones	Chapter 7	Jihad	"But the movement which is a natural outgrowth of the Islamic belief and which is the essence of the Islamic society does not let any individual hide himself. Every individual of this society must move! There should be a movement in his belief, a movement in his blood, a movement in his community, and in the structure of this organic society, and as the Jahiliyyah is all around him, and its residual influences in his mind and in the minds of those around him, the struggle goes on and the Jihad continues until the Day of Resurrection."
Qutb's Milestones	Chapter 9	Jihad	But any place where the Islamic Shari'ah is not enforced and where Islam is not dominant becomes the home of Hostility (Dar-ul-Harb) for both the Muslim and the Dhimmi. A Muslim will remain prepared to fight against it, whether it be his birthplace or a place where his relatives reside or where his property or any other material interests are located.
Qutb's Milestones	Chapter 9	Non-Muslims	There is only one place on earth which can be called the home of Islam (Dar-ul-Islam), and it is that place where the Islamic state is established and the Shari'ah is the authority and God's limits are observed, and where all the Muslims administer the affairs of the state with mutual consultation. The rest of the world is the home of hostility (Dar-ul-Harb). A Muslim can have only two possible relations with Dar-ul-Harb: peace with a contractual agreement, or war.
Tafsir Ibn Kathir	Vol. 1, P. 596; Sura 2:126--Al Baqarah	Jihad	In this Ayah, Allah made it obligatory for the Muslims to fight in Jihad against the evil of the enemy who transgress against Islam.
Tafsir Ibn Kathir	Vol. 2, P. 445-446; Sura 4:34--An Nisa	Women	Allah's statement, (beat them [wives]) means, if advice and ignoring her in bed do not produce the desired results, you are allowed to discipline them, without severe beating. ...you are allowed to discipline them lightly.

Source Document	Page Number/ Location	Subject Matter	Excerpt*
Tafsir Ibn Kathir	Vol. 2, P. 516; Sura 4:76--An Nisa	Jihad	Therefore, the believers fight in obedience to Allah and to gain His pleasure, while the disbelievers fight in obedience to Shaytan [Satan]. Allah then encourages the believers to fight His enemies. (So, fight against the friends of Shaytan; even feeble indeed is the plot of Shaytan).
Tafsir Ibn Kathir	Vol. 2, P. 519; Sura 4:77--An Nisa	Jihad	Rather, you will earn your full rewards for them [your good deeds]. This promise directs the focus of believers [Muslims] away from this life and makes them eager for the Hereafter, all the while encouraging them to fight in Jihad.
Tafsir Ibn Kathir	Vol. 3, P. 170; Sura 5:35--Al Ma-idah	Jihad	...He [Allah] commanded them [Muslims] to fight against their enemies, the disbelievers and idolators who have deviated from the straight path and abandoned the correct religion.
Tafsir Ibn Kathir	Vol. 4, P. 315; Sura 8:39--Al-Anfal	Non-Muslims	I [Muhammad] was commanded to fight against the people until they proclaim, "There is no deity worthy of worship except Allah."
Tafsir Ibn Kathir	Vol. 4, P. 376; Sura 9:5--At-Tawbah	Non-Muslims	Upon the end of the four months during which We prohibited you from fighting the idolators, and which is the grace period We gave them, then fight and kill the idolators wherever you may find them.
Tafsir Ibn Kathir	Vol. 4, P. 376; Sura 9:5--At-Tawbah	Non-Muslims	...[D]o not wait until you find them [idolators]. Rather, seek and besiege them in their areas and forts, gather intelligence about them in the various roads and fairways so that what is made wide looks ever smaller to them. This way, they will have no choice, but to die or embrace Islam[.]
Tafsir Ibn Kathir	Vol. 4, P. 408; Sura 9:30-31--At-Tawbah	Non-Muslims	Allah the Exalted encourages the believers [Muslims] to fight against the polytheists, disbelieving Jews and Christians, who uttered this terrible statement and utter lies against Allah, the Exalted.
Tafsir Ibn Kathir	Vol. 4, P. 475; Sura 9:73--At-Tawbah	Non-Muslims	Allah commanded the Prophet to fight the disbelievers with the sword, to strive against the hypocrites with the tongue and annulled lenient treatment of them.
Tafsir Ibn Kathir	Vol. 4, P. 475; Sura 9:73--At-Tawbah	Non-Muslims	Perform Jihad against the disbelievers with the sword and be harsh with the hypocrites with words, and this is the Jihad performed against them.
Tafsir Ibn Kathir	Vol. 4, P. 546; Sura 9:123--At-Tawbah	Non-Muslims	Allah commands the believers [Muslims] to fight the disbelievers, the closest in area to the Islamic state, then the farthest.
Tafsir Ibn Kathir	Vol. 4, P. 548; Sura 9:123--At-Tawbah	Non-Muslims	...fight the disbelievers and trust in Allah knowing that Allah is with you if you fear and obey Him.
Tafsir Ibn Kathir	Vol. 9, P. 23-24; Sura 45:14--Al-Jathiyah	Non-Muslims	In the beginning of Islam, Muslims were ordered to observe patience in the face of oppression of the idolators and the People of the Scriptures so that their hearts may incline towards Islam. However, when the disbelievers persisted in stubbornness, Allah legislated for the believers to fight in Jihad.

Source Document	Page Number/ Location	Subject Matter	Excerpt*
Tafsir Ibn Kathir	Vol. 9, P. 87; Sura 47:4-- Muhammad	Non-Muslims	(So, when you meet those who disbelieve (in battle), smite their necks) which means, 'when you fight against them [disbelievers], cut them down totally with your swords." ([U]ntil you have fully defeated them,) meaning, 'you have killed and utterly destroyed them.'
Tafsir Ibn Kathir	Vol. 9, P. 89; Sura 47:4-- Muhammad	Non-Muslims	He [Allah] has ordered Jihad and fighting against the enemies in order to try you and test your affairs.
Tafsir Ibn Kathir	Vol. 10, P. 72; Sura 66:9--At-Tarhim	Non-Muslims	Allah the Exalted orders His Messenger to perform Jihad against the disbelievers and hypocrites, the former with weapons and armaments and the later by establishing Allah's legislated penal code[.]
Riyad-us-Saliheen	Chapter 34:274	Women	Although Islam has permitted man, in inevitable circumstances, to rebuke his wife, it has also suggested a very wise course for it. It has suggested that first of all he should advise and preach [to] her, and if she does not mend her ways by these means, then he should stop sleeping with her, which is a great warning for the sensible wife. If she does not improve even by this method, then he may take recourse to slight beating, but in that he must avoid her head and face. He should take recourse to beating if he thinks that it would work, otherwise it is better to avoid it. But surprisingly enough some start the process of reformation with beating and that too with great ruthlessness which has not been permitted by Islam in any case. It is this aspect which the Prophet (PBUH) has highlighted in this Hadith. He has contended that when the wife is indispensable for man and it is very difficult for him to pass night without her then why should he beat her like a slave or bondmaid? He should try to understand that she, too, has feelings and her position is like one of the two wheels of the cart of life. If at all it comes to beating her then he must keep her true status in view before taking recourse to it. He should never loose sight of her importance in conjugal life.
Riyad-us-Saliheen	Chapter 34:276	Women	`Amr bin Al-Ahwas Al-Jushami (May Allah be pleased with him) reported that he had heard the Prophet (PBUH) saying on his Farewell Pilgrimage, after praising and glorifying Allah and admonishing people, "Treat women kindly, they are like captives in your hands; you do not owe anything else from them. In case they are guilty of open indecency, then do not share their beds and beat them lightly but if they return to obedience, do not have recourse to anything else against them.
Riyad-us-Saliheen	Chapter 234:1287-1288	Jihad	The Hadith points out the superiority of fighting in the way of Allah. The moment one fights for Allah's sake, be it in the early morning or the evening, is better than the world and all that is in it.
Riyad-us-Saliheen	Chapter 234:1289	Jihad	It [Haddith] brings into focus the excellence of fighting Jihad with one's wealth and life for the sake of Allah.

Source Document	Page Number/ Location	Subject Matter	Excerpt*
Riyad-us-Saliheen	Chapter 234:1290	Jihad	This Hadith highlights the excellence of observing Ribat [guarding the Islamic frontier for the sake of Allah] and fighting in the way of Allah. It also highlights the insignificance of this world and the great reward in the Hereafter which can be attained through Jihad.
Riyad-us-Saliheen	Chapter 234:1298	Jihad	The example cited here [in this Haddith] means that so long a Mujahid is engaged in Jihad, he is like a person who keeps himself occupied in Salat [prayer] at night and observes Saum [fasting] in the day time. The action of such a person can be equal in reward to the conduct of a Mujahid. Thus, in special situations Jihad is the most meritorious act. A worshipper cannot attain that reward for his worship which a Mujahid achieves in Jihad.
Riyad-us-Saliheen	Chapter 234:1308	Jihad	This Hadith also stresses the fact that if a person is unable to take part in Jihad due to illness, for example, he should then provide such material to a Mujahid which is helpful for him in Jihad. If he does so, he will be eligible to the same reward which is due on Jihad. This would also be a source of increase and growth in his possessions.
Riyad-us-Saliheen	Chapter 234:1319	Jihad	Jannat-ul-Firdaus is the highest portion of Jannah[Paradise]. The allocation of this portion [of Paradise] to the martyrs is a proof that Jihad is very much liked by Allah.
Riyad-us-Saliheen	Chapter 234:1345	Jihad	What this Hadith really means is that when the situation calls for Jihad then the foremost priority of a Muslim should be Jihad. In such an event his passion for touring the world should yield to the spirit of Jihad against the infidels and then he must with his full force fight against the enemy.
Riyad-us-Saliheen	Chapter 234:1348	Jihad	This Hadith means that one who neither takes part in Jihad nor provides arms to a Mujahid nor looks after the families of the Mujahidun during their absence, is guilty of crimes for which he is punished in this world by Allah. It is, therefore, the duty of the Muslim Ummah [community] that it should in no way neglect the obligation of Jihad and all its requirements; otherwise it will suffer punishment in this world and in the next.
Riyad-us-Saliheen	Chapter 234:1349	Jihad	This Hadith mentions three categories of Jihad, namely Jihad with wealth, Jihad with one's life and Jihad by speech. One should make Jihad as is warranted by the situation one is confronted with. That is, where a Muslim is required to sacrifice his life, he must sacrifice his life; where he is required to sacrifice his wealth, he should spend wealth; and where he is required to make Jihad by means of his speech, he should do it by speech. One should not hesitate to spend for the sake of Allah what is required by the situation.

Source Document	Page Number/ Location	Subject Matter	Excerpt*
Riyad-us-Saliheen	Chapter 234:1352	Jihad	The Ahadith mentioned in this chapter make the importance of Jihad and the reason for so much stress on it abundantly clear. These also show how great a crime it is to ignore it. It is very unfortunate indeed that present-day Muslims are guilty of renouncing Jihad in every part of the world. May Allah help us to overcome this negligence.
Maududi's Jihad in Islam	P. 18	Jihad	These [Muslim] men who propagate religion are not mere preachers or missionaries, but the functionaries of God, (so that they may be witnesses for the people), and it is their duty to wipe out oppression, mischief, strife, immorality, high handedness and unlawful exploitation from the world by force of arms.
Maududi's Jihad in Islam	P. 20	Jihad	If these people [Muslims] evade their duty of actively striving for this end [imposing an Islamic government], it clearly implies that they are hypocrites and liars in their faith.
Maududi's Jihad in Islam	P. 20	Jihad	In these words, the Qur'an has given a clear and definite decree that the acid test of the true devotion of a party to its convictions is whether or not it expends all its resources of wealth and life in the struggle for installing its faith as the ruling power in the State.
The Meaning of the Quran	Sura 2--Al-Baqarah	Jihad	Salat, Fast, Zakat, Haj and Jihad have been prescribed for the moral training of the Ummat [Muslim community].
The Meaning of the Quran	Sura 4--An-Nisa	Women	If the wife is defiant and does [n]ot obey her husband or does not guard his rights, three measures have been mentioned, but it does not mean that all the three are to be taken at one and the same time. Though these have been permitted, they are to be administered with a sense of proportion according to the nature and extent of the offense. [I]f a mere light admonition proves effective, there is no need to resort to a severer step. As to a beating, the Holy Prophet allowed it very reluctantly and even then did not like it. But the fact is that there are certain women who do not mend their ways without a beating. In such a case, the Holy Prophet has instructed that she would not be beaten on the face, or cruelly, or with anything which might leave a mark on the body.
The Meaning of the Quran	Sura 4--An-Nisa	Jihad	In the sight of Allah, there are two distinct parties of fighters. One party is that of the Believers who fight for the cause of Allah in order to establish his way on His earth, and every sincere Believer is bound to perform this duty.

Source Document	Page Number/ Location	Subject Matter	Excerpt*
The Meaning of the Quran	Surah 5--Al-Ma-idah	Jihad	Thus, this verse exhorts the Believer to fight his enemies on all fronts. On one side, he confronts Satan and a host of his followers, and on the second, his own self and its alluring temptations. On the third side, he has to fight many people who have swerved from the way of God, and with whom he is bound by close social, cultural and economic relations. On the fourth side, he is required to oppose all those religious, cultural and political systems that are founded on rebellion against God and force people to submit to falsehood instead of the Truth. Though these enemies employ different weapons, they all have one and the same object in view, that is, to subdue their victims and bring them under their own subjection. It is obvious that true success can only be achieved if one becomes wholly and solely a servant of God and obeys Him openly and also secretly, to the exclusion of obedience to all others. Thus there is bound to be a conflict with all the [f]our enemies: Therefore the Believer cannot achieve his object unless he engages himself with all these hostile and opposing forces at one and the same time and at all events, and removing all these hindrances marches onwards on the way of Allah.
The Meaning of the Quran	Sura 8--Al-Anfal	Jihad	This aim [of Islamic warfare] has two aspects-- the negative and the positive. On the negative side, the aim of war is to abolish (fitnah), and on the positive, it is to establish Allah's Way completely and in its entirety. This is the only objective for which it is lawful, nay, obligatory for the believers to fight.
The Meaning of the Quran	Sura 9--At-Taubah	Non-Muslims	In this portion [verses 13-37] the Muslims have been urged to fight in the Way of Allah with the mushrik [polytheistic] Arabs, the Jews and the Christians, who were duly warned of the consequences of their mischievous and inimical behavior.
The Meaning of the Quran	Sura 9--At-Taubah	Non-Muslims	"The second reason why Jihad should be waged against them is [th]at they did not adopt the Law sent down by Allah through His Messenger. [Humiliation/reduction in status] is the aim of Jihad with the Jews and the Christians and it is not to force them to become Muslims and adopt the 'Islamic Way of Life.' They should be forced to pay Jizyah [poll tax] in order to put an end to their independence and supremacy so that they should not remain rulers and sovereigns in the land. These powers should be wrested from them by the followers of the true Faith, who should assume the sovereignty and lead others towards the Right Way, while they [Jews and Christians] should become their subjects and pay jizyah."

Source Document	Page Number/ Location	Subject Matter	Excerpt*
The Meaning of the Quran	Sura 9--At-Taubah	Non-Muslims	This Command [to fight the unbelievers and hypocrites] enunciated the change of policy towards the hypocrites. Up to this time, leniency was being shown to them for two reasons. First, the Muslims had not as yet become so powerful as to take the risk of an internal conflict in addition to the one with the external enemies. The other reason was to give trough (sic) respite to those people who were involved in doubts and suspicions so that they could get sufficient time for attaining to faith and belief. But now the time had come f[o]r a change of policy. The whole of Arabia had been subdued and a bitter conflict with the external enemies was about to start; therefore it was required that these internal enemies should be crushed down so that they should not be able to conspire with the external enemies to stir up any internal danger to the Muslims. And now it had become possible to crush them. As regards [t]he second reason, these hypocrites had been given respite for a period of nine years to observe, to consider and test the Right Way, and they could have availed of it, if they had any good in them. So there was no reason why any more leniency should be shown to them. Therefore, Allah enjoined the Muslims to treat the hypocrites on one and the same level with the disbelievers and start Jihad against them, and to give up the policy of leniency [th]ey had adopted towards them and adopt a fine and stern policy instead.
The Meaning of the Quran	Sura 9--At-Taubah	Non-Muslims	From the apparent wording of this verse, it may be inferred that only those Muslims have at first been held responsible to fight with those enemies of Islam who live near their territory. But if we read this verse along with the succeeding passage, it becomes clear that here "disbelievers who are near you refers to those hypocrites who were doing great harm to to Islamic Society by mixing up with the sincere Muslims. This very thing was stated in v. 73 at the beginning of this discourse. The Command has been repeated at its end in order to impress on the Muslims the importance of the matter and to urge them to do Jihad and crush these internal enemies, without paying the Least regard to the racial, family and social relations that had been proving a binding force with them.
The Meaning of the Quran	Sura 66--At-Tahrim	Non-Muslims	The commentary referred the reader to the author's previous comment from Sura 9--At-Taubah located in cell "D-272."

Appendix B - Shariʻa-Adherent Behaviors: [1]

List	Description	Observation: Yes/No or Count	Subject to Secondary Review
Gender Segregation During Prayer Service	Shariʻa-adherent communal prayer occurs when men and women are segregated during prayer service. The segregation could occur by virtue of men and women praying in different buildings or different rooms. The segregation could also occur when men and women were in the same room, but were separated either with or without the use of a physical divider. Non-Shariʻa-adherent communal prayer occurs when men and women are not segregated during the prayer service and the genders mix.	Yes/No	No
Alignment of Men's Prayer Lines	Shariʻa-adherent alignment of men's prayer lines occurs when either the imam, lay leader, or the worshipers inspect and enforce the straightness of the men's prayer lines. Non-Shariʻa-adherent alignment of men's prayer lines occurs when there is no observable attention paid to strict alignment of the men's prayer lines.	Yes/No	No
Imam's or Lay Leader's Beard [3]	An imam's or lay leader's beard is a Sunna-style (i.e., full) beard, whether trimmed or not and either with or without henna dye coloring the beard. A non-Sunna style beard is either limited to a chin-beard or if the imam or lay leader wears no beard at all.	Yes/No	No

List	Description	Observation: Yes/No or Count	Subject to Secondary Review
Imam or Lay Leader Wore Head Covering	Shari'a-adherent behavior is that the imam or lay leader wore a religious head covering. Non-Shari'a adherent behavior is that the imam or lay leader did not wear a religious head covering	Yes/No	No
Imam's or Lay Leader's Clothing	Shari'a-adherent garb is any of the following: (a) short thoub; (b) pants rolled up above the ankles; or (c) ankle-length thoub. Non-Shari'a-adherent garb is Western-style clothing such as modern-style dress or casual pants and shirt.	Yes/No	No
Imam or Lay Leader Wore Watch on His Right Wrist [4]	Certain Salafists wear the watch on the right wrist. Wearing the watch on the left wrist or not wearing a watch at all.	Yes/No	No
Percentage of Men with Beards	Shari'a-adherent behavior is for an adult male worshiper to have a beard (full or not). Non-Shari'a-adherent behavior is for an adult male worshiper to not have a beard.	Count	No
Adult Male Worshipers' Clothing	Shari'a-adherent behavior is to wear either: (a) short thoub; (b) pants rolled up above the ankles; or (c) ankle-length thoub or similar Muslim attire. Non-Shari'a-adherent behavior is to wear Western-style clothing such as pants not rolled up above the ankles.	Count	No

List	Description	Observation: Yes/No or Count	Subject to Secondary Review
Adult Female Worshipers' Clothing	Shari'a-adherent behavior is to wear either the traditional hijab (covering the hair) or the niqab (covering the entire female body except the eyes). Non-Shari'a-adherent behavior is to wear the modern hijab (a scarf that does not completely cover the hair) or to not wear any hair covering.	Count	No
Girls (age 5-12) Wear Hijab	Shari'a-adherent behavior is to wear the traditional hijab. Non-Shari'a-adherent behavior is to not wear the hijab.	Count	No
Boys (age 5-12) Wear Head Covering	Shari'a-adherent behavior is to wear a religious head covering. Non-Shari'a-adherent behavior is to not wear a religious head covering.	Count	No
Presence of Violence-Positive Shari'a Legal and Religious Texts or Presence of Violence-Positive Islamic Political Literature	If the surveyor found the *Fiqh us Sunnah* or *Tafsir Ibn Kathir*, but not more extreme materials, then the mosque was categorized as containing moderate-rated material. If the surveyor found the *Riyadh us Salaheen*, works by Qutb or Mawdudi, or similar materials, then the mosque was categorized as containing severe-rated materials. If the surveyor found no violence-positive materials or if the violence-positive materials constituted less than 10% of all available materials, then the mosque was categorized as containing no materials.	Yes/No	No, unless the surveyor found materials promoting *Fiqh us Sunnah*, *Tafsir Ibn Kathir*, *Riyadh us Salaheen*, or works by Qutb or Mawdudi. Other materials were subject to a secondary review.

List	Description	Observation: Yes/No or Count	Subject to Secondary Review
Imam Recommended Studying Texts Promoting Violence	Following the prayer service, the surveyor asked the following question: "Do you recommend the study of: (a) only the Quran and/or Sunna; (b) Tafsir Ibn Kathir; (c) Fiqh Us Sunna; (e) Reliance of the Traveller; or (f) the works of Qutb, such as Milestones, and Maududi, such as The Meaning of the Quran?" If the Imam or lay leader recommended studying any of the above-mentioned materials except for the Quran and/or Sunna, then the Imam or lay leader was recorded as having recommended the study of texts promoting the rated material.	Yes/No	No.
Promoted Joining a Terrorist Organization [5]	If materials available on mosque premises promoted joining a known terrorist organization, such as "mujahideen" engaged in jihad abroad, then the mosque was recorded as having promoted joining a terrorist organization.	Yes/No	Yes
Promoted Financial Support of Terror	If materials available on mosque premises promoted the financial support of terrorism, jihadists, or terrorist organizations, then the mosque was recorded as having promoted the financial support of terror. Examples include materials that made explicit calls to support mujahideen abroad or families of Palestinian suicide bombers.	Yes/No	Yes

List	Description	Observation: Yes/No or Count	Subject to Secondary Review
Openly Collected Money at the Mosque for a Known Terrorist Organization	If materials available on mosque premises indicated that speakers came to the mosque to raise money for specific terrorist organizations, then the mosque was recorded as having openly collected money at the mosque for a known terrorist organization.	Yes/No	Yes
Promoted Establishment of the Islamic Caliphate in the U.S.	If materials available on mosque premises promoted establishing the Islamic Caliphate in the United States, then the mosque was recorded as having promoted the establishment of the Islamic Caliphate in the U.S.	Yes/No	Yes
Praised Terror Against the West	If materials available on mosque premises praised engaging in acts of violence against the West or praised acts of terrorism previously committed against the West, then the mosque was recorded as having praised terror against the West.	Yes/No	Yes
Mosque Invited Guest Imams or Preachers Known to Have Promoted Violent Jihad	If materials available at the mosque indicated that the mosque had invited a guest imam or other guest speaker who is known to have promoted violent jihad, then the mosque was recorded as having invited guest imams or preachers known to have promoted violent jihad. Examples of such imams include Siraj Wahhaj, Ayman al-Zawahiri, and Anwar al-Awlaki.	Yes/No	Yes

List	Description	Observation: Yes/No or Count	Subject to Secondary Review
Promoted Violent Jihad	If any of the materials featured on mosque property promoted engaging in terrorist activity; promoted the financial support of terrorism or jihadists; promoted the use of force, terror, war, and violence to implement Shari'a; promoted the idea that oppression and subversion of Islam should be changed by deed first, then by speech, then by faith; praised acts of terrorism against the West; or praised suicide bombers against Israelis, then the mosque was recorded as having promoted violent jihad.	Yes/No	Yes

Notes

[1] According to Islamic jurisprudence, Shari'a-adherence can be measured across several normative axes, such as obligatory-prohibited, recommended-discouraged, and simply permissible. In theory, every act of a Shari'a-adherent Muslim falls within one of the normative categories —that is, there is no behavior outside of Shari'a. For purposes of this survey, the authors have chosen, except where indicated by notation, the obligatory-prohibited and the recommended-discouraged or recommended-permissible axes, which we have demarcated Shari'a adherent/non-Shari'a adherent, respectively.

[2] If a mosque, on the basis of materials observed by the surveyor, was recorded as having: (a) promoted violent jihad; (b) promoted joining a terrorist organization; (c) promoted financial support of terror; (d) collected money openly at the mosque for a known terrorist organization; (e) promoted establishing the Caliphate in the U.S.; (f) praised terror against the West; (g) distributed memorabilia featuring jihadists or terrorist organizations; or (h) invited imams or preachers who are known to have promoted violent jihad, then the materials that the surveyor relied on to record the presence of this material were subject to a secondary review by a committee of three subject-matter experts. This secondary review was collected and reviewed by the experts evaluating the materials independently of one another. A consensus view of two of the three experts was required to confirm the surveyor's observation. In 63% of the cases, the materials were so explicit in their promotion, praise, or support for the above behaviors that the committee's decision was unanimous. In no instance was there not a consensus and agreement with the surveyor's observation.

[3] The different legal schools vary on whether a beard is obligatory or preferable; they also differ on whether the beard for purposes of fiqh is only the chin hairs or also the lateral hairs of the sideburns and cheeks; and they differ on the minimum required length before trimming is permitted. The majority view, taking into account all schools and the Salafist opinions, is that a full beard is Sunna (following the behavior of Muhammad) and if not obligatory, preferable. For purposes of this survey, the full beard, trimmed or not, was considered Shari'a adherent and a chin beard or no beard, was considered as non-Sunna, and in the survey's lexicon, non-adherent.

[4] While wearing a watch on the right hand is not strictly speaking a Shari'a requirement, during the preparation of the methodology of this survey, the authors identified literature at several mosques attended by Salafists advocating the wearing of a watch on the right hand for two

reasons: not to wear jewelry on the left hand to follow the mode of dress of Muhammad, who, based upon certain Sunna, did not wear jewelry on his left hand; and to avoid dressing in the way of non-Muslims. The authors decided to add this observation to determine whether this behavior translated into observance by the more fundamentalist Salafists. They also observed that the 12 imams who wore the watch on the right hand were right handed.

[5]All of the materials characterized from this point to the end of the survey was dated or produced prior to September 11, 2001; but was still available at or sold by the mosque in prominent fashion.

Appendix C - Data Tables

Table 1: Number of mosques surveyed by state		
	n=	Percent
Arizona	2	2.0
California	26	26.0
District of Columbia	1	1.0
Florida	12	12.0
Georgia	1	1.0
Michigan	8	8.0
New Jersey	5	5.0
New York	3	3.0
North Carolina	12	12.0
Pennsylvania	1	1.0
South Carolina	2	2.0
Tennessee	2	2.0
Texas	9	9.0
Utah	3	3.0
Virginia	13	13.0
Total	100	100.0

Table 2: Association of strictness of violence-positive materials available at mosque and key aspects of sharia-based mosque prayer service and sharia-based imam characteristics

	No material (n=19)	Moderate [1] (n=30)	Severe (n=51) [2]	Total	Chi-square (all df=2)
Prayer service [3] Segregation in prayer					6.48, p=.04
No	16 (26%)	17 (27%)	29 (47%)	62	
Yes	2 (5%)	13 (35%)	22 (60%)	37	
Alignment of prayer lines					16.86, p≤.001
No	16 (36%)	10 (22%)	19 (42%)	45	
Yes	2 (4%)	20 (37%)	32 (59%)	54	
Description of imam or lay leader [4] Imam or lay leader has Sunna beard					
No [5]	13 (26%)	14 (28%)	23 (46%)	50	6.62, p=.04
Yes [6]	3 (7%)	15 (33%)	28 (61%)	46	
Imam wore head covering					
No	9 (20%)	16 (35%)	21 (46%)	46	1.98, p=.37
Yes	7 (14%)	13 (26%)	30 (60%)	50	
Imam wore traditional (non-Western garb)					4.97, p=.08
No	11 (25%)	14 (32%)	19 (43%)	44	
Yes	5 (10%)	15 (29%)	32 (62%)	52	
Imam wore watch on right wrist [7]					2.61, p=.27
No	15 (18%)	23 (28%)	45 (54%)	83	
Yes	1 (8%)	6 (50%)	5 (42%)	12	

[1] Has only Tafsir Ibn Kathir commentary on the Qur'an and/or Fiqh-us-Sunnah (n=20).
[2] Has Riyadh-us-Salaheen (n=7) or more extreme fiqh material.
[3] In 1 mosque there was no prayer and surveyor could not determine the usual practice.
[4] 4 mosques did not have a leader.
[5] 3 with no beard included in this category.
[6] 3 had traditional beards with henna; and all were in the severe group. They were combined with this group for ease of reporting.
[7] In 1 case it was not determined.

Table 3: Association of strictness of violence-positive materials available at mosque and mosque attendance and key sharia-based worshiper characteristics

	No material (n=19)	Moderate [8] (n=30)	Severe [9] (n=51)	Total	F test (unless otherwise noted)
Number of worshipers [10]	Median 4 Mean 15	Median 25 Mean 60	Median 45 Mean 118	Median 28 Mean 81	Kruskal-Wallis, p≤.002
Percentage of men with beards (SD) [11]	14% (26.3) (n=17)	36% (25.4) (n=30)	48% (32.4) (n=51)	39% (31.7) (n=98)	F=8.61, df=2, 95 P≤.001
Percentage of men with hats	16% (25.8) (n=17)	34% (26.2) (n=29)	47% (32.6) (n=51)	38% (31.3) (n=97)	F=6.54, df=2, 94 p=.002
Percentage of men with Western garb	73% (39.9) (n=16)	35% (30.7) (n=30)	34% (33.1) (n=51)	41% (36.2) (n=97)	F=8.79, df=2, 94 p≤.001
Percentage of women with modern hijab (vs. traditional hijab/niqab) [12]	57% (45.0) (n=7)	38% (37.5) (n=21)	42% (27.3) (n=37)	33% (32.9) (n=65)	F=0.92, df=2, 62, p=.40
Percentage of girls with hijab	29% (48.8) (n=7)	14% (32.2) (n=21)	36% (40.4) (n=37)	28% (43.8) (n=65)	F=1.87, df=2,62 p=.16
Percentage of boys with head covering [13]	14% (37.8) (n=7)	24% (37.6) (n=20)	32% (40) (n=36)	27% (38.8) (n=63)	F=0.72, df=2, 60, p=.49

[8]Has only Tafsir Ibn Kathir commentary on the Qur'an and/or Fiqh-us-Sunnah (n=20).
[9] Has Riyadh-us-Salaheen (n=7) or more extreme fiqh material.
[10] In 2 mosques only the imam was present.
[11] Data in parentheses that follow percentage figures denote the standard deviation.
[12] Women were present in 65 mosques.
[13] Boys were present in 63 mosques.

Table 4: Association of key sharia-based aspects of mosque prayer service and sharia-based imam characteristics and imam recommending violence-positive material				
	Did not recommend [14] (n=15, 15%)	Recommended (n=82, 85%)	Total (n=97)[15]	Chi-square (all df=1) p=
Prayer service Segregation in prayer				
No	12 (20%)	48 (80%)	60	3.77, p=.05
Yes	2 (6%)	34 (94%)	36	
Alignment of prayer lines				
No	12 (28%)	31 (72%)	43	11.10, p=.001
Yes	2 (4%)	51 (96%)	53	
Description of imam or lay leader Beard of imam or lay leader				
No	11 (22%)	39 (78%)	50	4.61, p=.03
Yes	3 (7%)	43 (93%)	46	
Imam wore head covering				
No	9 (20%)	37 (80%)	46	1.76, p=.18
Yes	5 (10%)	45 (90%)	50	
Imam wore traditional garb				
No	10 (23%)	34 (77%)	44	4.32, p=.04
Yes	4 (8%)	48 (92%)	52	
Imam wore watch on right wrist [16]				
No	14 (17%)	69 (83%)	83	2.37, p=.12
Yes	0 (0%)	12 (100%)	12	

[14] Ten imams did not recommend that a worshiper study any violence-positive materials and 4 imams instructed against the study of violence-positive materials. All 14 observations were included in the "do not recommend" category.
[15] In 4 mosques, neither an imam nor a lay leader was present. However, in 1 of these 4 cases the imam had made clear recommendations on the mosque's webpage.
[16] In 1 case it was not determined.

Table 5: Association of mosque attendance and key sharia-based worshiper characteristics and imam recommending violence-positive material			
	Did not recommend [17] (n=15, 15%)	Recommended (n=82, 85%)	F test for significance
Number of worshipers	Median=4 Total=250	Median=39 Total=7864	Mann-Whitney U p≤.001
Percentage of men with beards (SD) [18]	13% (27.6) (n=13)	44% (30.3) (n=82)	F=11.99, df=1, 93, p=.001
Percentage of men with hats	15% (27.2) (n=13)	42% (30.4) (n=81)	F=9.07, df=1, 92, p=.003
Percentage of men with Western garb	87% (19.1) (n=12)	34% (32.6) (n=82)	F=30.17, df=1, 91, p<.0001
Percentage of women with modern hijab (vs.traditional hijab/niqab) [19]	70% (44.7) (n=5)	41% (30.9) (n=59)	F=3.85, df=1, 62, p≤.054
Percentage of girls with hijab	20% (44.7%) (n=5)	29% (41.6) (n=60)	F=.21, df=1, 63, p=.65
Percentage of boys with head coverings	0% (n=5)	30% (39.6) (n=58)	F=2.77, df=1, 91, p<.10

[17] Ten imams did not recommend the study of any materials and 4 imams instructed against the study of violence-positive materials. All 14 observations were included in the "do not recommend" category.
[18] Data in parentheses that follow percentage figures denote the standard deviation.
[19] Women were present in 65 mosques. Data collected on percent women with niqab (rare), hijab, and modern hijab.

Table 6: Association of strictness of violence-positive materials available at mosque and promotion of violent jihad					
	No material (n=19)	Moderate [20] (n=30)	Severe [21] (n=51)	Total (n=100)	Chi-square (all df=2)
Imam recommended studying texts promoting violence					70.7, p≤.001
No	14 (82%)	1 (3%)	0 (0%)	15	
Yes	3 (18% [22])	28 (97%)	51 (100%)	82	
Promoted violent jihad					87.6, p≤.001
No	18 (95%)	1 (3%)	0 (0%)	19	
Yes	1 (5%)	29 (97%)	51 (100%)	81	
Promoted joining terrorist organization					.49, p=.78
No	18 (95%)	28 (93%)	46 (90%)	92	
Yes	1 (5%)	2 (7%)	5 (10%)	8	
Promoted financial support of terror					81.9, p≤.001
No	18 (95%)	1 (3%)	1 (2%)	20	
Yes	1 (5%)	29 (97%)	50 (98%)	80	
Collected money openly at mosque for known terrorist organization					.70, p=.70
No	18 (95%)	29 (97%)	47 (92%)	94	
Yes	1 (5%)	1 (3%)	4 (8%)	6	
Promotes Caliphate in US					81.9, p≤.001
No	18 (95%)	1 (3%)	1 (2%)	20	
Yes	1 (5%)	29 (97%)	50 (98%)	80	
Praising terror against West					87.6, p≤.001
No	18 (95%)	1 (3%)	0 (0%)	19	
Yes	1 (5%)	29 (97%)	51 (100%)	81	
Distributed memorabilia featuring jihadists or terrorist organizations					0.99, p=.61
No	18 (95%)	28 (93%)	45 (88%)	91	
Yes	1 (5%)	2 (7%)	6 (12%)	9	
Mosque invited imams or preachers who are known to have promoted violent jihad					28.9, p≤.001
No	18 (95%)	12 (40%)	12 (24%)	42	
Yes	1 (5%)	18 (60%)	39 (76%)	58	

[20] Has only Tafsir Ibn Kathir commentary on the Qur'an and/or Fiqh-us-Sunnah (n=20).
[21] Has Riyadh-us-Salaheen (n=7) or more extreme fiqh material.
[22] Denominator is 17, 2 in this column had no imam or leader.

113

www.ingramcontent.com/pod-product-compliance
Lightning Source LLC
Chambersburg PA
CBHW070905180526
45168CB00005B/1939